Joy COMES IN THE MORNING

CYNDI FOSTER

Impact Christian Books, Inc.
Kirkwood, MO 63122

Joy Comes in the Morning
by Cyndi Foster
ISBN 0-89228-129-4
Library of Congress Catalog Card Number: Pending
Copyright ©1996 by Cyndi Foster

Published by:
Impact Christian Books, Inc.
332 Leffingwell Ave.,
Kirkwood, MO 63122
314-822-3309
(Formerly published by Bridge-Logos under ISBN 0-88270-729-9)

Dedication

Therefore we also, since we are surrounded by so great a cloud of witnesses, let us lay aside every weight, and the sin which so easily ensnares us, and let us run with endurance the race that is set before us,

looking unto Jesus, the author and finisher of our faith, who for the joy that was set before Him endured the cross, despising the shame, and has sat down at the right hand of the throne of God.

Hebrews 12:1-2

In Loving Memory

Kristie Renee' Porter
(September 1978 - September 1986)

Nicolas Samuel Arnold
(December 1987 - January 1992)

Lauren Elizabeth Foster
(September 1984 - May 1992)

Latoya Yvonne Parham
(March 1979 - July 1993)

Christopher Wade Buchanan
(April 1967 - August 1993)

Nathaniel Reid Smith
(September 1977 - June 1994)

Crystal Dawn Dicus
(February 1976 - April 1995)

Aimee Marie Busic
(February 1992 - May 1995)

Acknowledgements

Special Thanks To:

My husband, John, and our two sons, Mitchell and Michael, for their loving support. I love you.

Also to Donna Fox, Ginny Turco, and Laurie Zeigler for their editorial help.

Table of Contents

Section One

Lauren Elizabeth Foster

(September 22, 1984 - May 23, 1992)

1

Why, Lord?

I stood in the hospital room with a million thoughts circulating through my mind: *Lord, why is that precious little boy dead? How did I fail You and this family that depended on me to bring the good news of the Gospel into their son's fight against leukemia? Lord, I don't understand why that child was supernaturally healed just weeks ago and now he is dead.*

Yet with all my questions I knew that one thing remained unchanged—God is faithful and His Word is true:

> For what if some did not believe? Will their unbelief make the faithfulness of God without effect?
>
> Certainly not! Indeed, let God be true but every man a liar.
>
> Romans 3:3-4a

With tears streaming down my face I walked down ᴛe hospital corridor and away from the room. The boy's young mother had desperately clung to the hope of Jesus as the healer, and now her dream of seeing her son well was shattered. Less than fifteen minutes earlier, he had died in my arms. As the life support was removed from his body, he never took a breath.

Because I had felt the presence of God and had seen His hand move so mightily during the initial onslaught of little Nicolas Arnold's illness, I had felt certain that God would answer this family's prayer for his complete healing. To the best of her knowledge, Nicolas's mother spoke the Word and believed the teaching she had recently heard concerning the authority of the believer. One month earlier, just after the Christmas holiday, I had prayed a powerful prayer for this little boy. The following week, Nicolas left the hospital in an astounding full remission! They shared a wonderful late Christmas celebration.

Then the cancer suddenly returned and this small child suffered immensely and fell into a coma. Although the physicians declared Nicolas brain dead, they granted his parents, Sam and Carla Arnold, permission to keep him on life support. They were believing God for a miracle.

Now it was over—but how could that be?

Less than five hours earlier, it seemed as though God was answering our prayer of faith. Carla declared the Word of the Lord and refused to look at the tragic circumstances before her. Suddenly, the Holy Spirit was touching Nicolas's body. The monitors on the life support machines were showing unusual patterns. Carla, who was a nurse, was ecstatic as she explained to me that life was returning to her son. The presence of the Holy Spirit was so powerful that it felt as if a blanket settled over the room.

Putting my faith to the test, the Holy Spirit spoke within my heart. His command was clear—I was to lock the door and stop anyone from entering the room. As I spoke the instruction to Nicolas's mother, we both panicked. What would the hospital staff do if we locked the door? We froze. Within seconds, the attending physician entered the room. As he took a step toward the patient, the monitors immediately returned to their original position. The miracle didn't take place. All my faith had turned to doubt and fear. Five hours later Nicolas was officially pronounced dead.

I left the hospital and walked through the dark to my car. The cold winter air bit at my face. I had walked into my wilderness. I knew that God couldn't fail, but, somehow, I knew, I had failed. Christian books, as valuable and anointed as they sometimes are, could not give me the answers I needed—only the Holy Spirit could help me. As much as I could I submitted my contrite heart and broken spirit to God, trusting that by His Spirit I would learn the truth about genuine faith. "The Lord is near to those who have a broken heart, And saves such as have a contrite spirit" (Psalms 34:18).

Still, I doubted that God could ever use me again. I even prayed that He wouldn't. The apostle Peter wrote ". . . be clothed with humility, for 'God resists the proud, But gives grace to the humble.' Therefore humble yourselves under the mighty hand of God, . . ." (1 Peter 5:5-6). So I did all I could to crucify my flesh and humble myself before God. If the Lord ever sent me to minister again, I knew it would have to be through His power and anointing, and not solely based on my knowledge of His Word.

5

As I made the hour drive home from the hospital, my thoughts went back to almost two years ago to the day. My sister and her husband, Donna and Ron Ferguson, had also walked down that very same hospital corridor. Their son, Andrew, however, was leaving with them. After spending the first ten months of his life in the hospital with little or no medical hope for recovery, Andrew was being released, and the physicians were delighted. They had been certain that he would never leave their facility alive. His miraculous turnaround stunned the medical community. Both Donna and I knew it was the promise of God coming to pass. The doctors could not guarantee what lay ahead for baby Andrew, nevertheless, Donna was optimistic.

During Andrew's illness, The Holy Spirit had revealed to me the truths in the Scriptures concerning healing, faith, authority, and the power of God's Word. Furthermore, He led me to many anointed faith teachers. I have the highest respect for these men and women who teach a message that many prefer to dismiss as a false gospel. Although accounts of supernatural manifestations fill the pages of the Bible, many disregard any revelation that does not agree with their religious traditions or experiences. However, I know that the Most High God taught me through several faith teachers.

Andrew was healed because of my sister's obedience when the Holy Spirit told her to learn the faith message and apply it to her son's situation. Although I appreciate the truth of the salvation message, it is wonderful to know that God has provided a way for us to live in victory during our lifetimes.

Too many times we're satisfied with the "milk" of the Scriptures. The same Scriptures also command us to desire the deeper truths:

> For though by this time you ought to be teachers, you need someone to teach you again the first principles of the oracles of God; and you have come to need milk and not solid food.
>
> For everyone who partakes only of milk is unskilled in the word of righteousness, for he is a babe.
>
> But solid food belongs to those who are of full age, that is, those who by reason of use have their senses exercised to discern both good and evil.
>
> Hebrews 5:12-14

How many of us today want to know all the truths in the Word? Many of us may feel that our church is already teaching the whole Gospel message, but look at the following list of teachings that the writer of Hebrews considers to be the *elementary principles* of Christ:

> Therefore, leaving the discussion of the elementary principles of Christ, let us go on to perfection, not laying again the foundation of repentance from dead works and of faith toward God, of the doctrine of baptisms, of laying on of hands, of resurrection of the dead, and of eternal judgment.
>
> Hebrews 6:1-2

Sometimes our church doctrines don't teach even these elementary truths. Yet Hosea 4:6 tells us that God Himself declared, "My people are destroyed for lack of knowledge."

After listening to a number of faith teachings, I was determined to discover for myself if healing was a covenant promise for my sister's baby, Andrew. I read every passage in the Bible concerning sickness and death. After researching the Word, I knew that God's will was to heal His people.

Andrew was born prematurely with a hole in his esophagus. Although he weighed only three pounds making any surgery extremely risky, the doctors said it was essential that they operate immediately. We hoped for complete success, but during the operation his stomach was punctured. This and other complications led to his lungs collapsing. The future looked hopeless for Andrew. In addition to being diagnosed as a chronic lung baby, he had a high probability of having many major disabilities.

Andrew was one of twin boys. Unlike Andrew, his brother, Ryan, also born prematurely of course, was now in perfect health. Many who were praying in faith for little Andrew's recovery felt that Ryan was the perfect vision for God's will for Andrew. Every time Donna looked at baby Ryan she captured his image in her spirit. She knew that Andrew was to one day look identical to his twin. In keeping with His Word, the Lord was faithful to pour out His grace in this situation.

God supernaturally encouraged us through words of prophecy, tapes, books, and sermons. Although Andrew's miracle is an ongoing process, we have seen God's hand in his life and we know that one day he will be just as whole as his identical twin, Ryan.

8

Now little Nicolas had died even after many of the same kinds of prayers. As I pulled into my driveway, many thoughts coursed through my mind. *Why did one child receive healing when the medical community had given up all hope, and the other one die in my arms? What had caused God to heal this child in the beginning and then allow the disease to return?* I needed to find the answers to these tough questions.

My journey for truth had taken an unexpected turn with the death of little Nicolas.

2

Teach Me Your Ways

Tears of sorrow and grief filled my days. I felt as if I were experiencing the pain of Nicolas's parents. I knew that Satan had come to destroy this family. As I cried out to God for understanding, He began to reveal to me the areas where I missed His leading. He pointed out the reasons I was sent to minister to this family. At our first meeting, Nicolas's father confessed Christ as his Savior. Sitting on his son's hospital bed, Sam invited Christ into his heart. Witnessing his father's salvation thrilled little Nicolas and he smiled from ear to ear. His parents' marriage had been a bit rocky, and it began to be restored immediately after his father's commitment to Christ.

During my second visit to the hospital, Nicolas's mother, Carla, received the baptism of the Holy Spirit. This deeper walk helped her survive the death of her son. Standing with this family as they fought the fight of faith, was the purpose for my being sent to them. God's desire was to stop the enemy from destroying a family. Only God can heal. He knew my limitations when He sent me to minister to Nicolas.

My sorrow and despair lifted as I understood my purpose for being sent. We can't choose to go only to the easy places, or the places where the results are always what *we* want them to be. Realizing this, I surrendered to God's will for my life. Wherever He sent me I would go, and do only what He wanted me to do.

Finally, I was at peace with Nicolas's death. Now I hungered to know more about God and His ways. Previously I had thought Andrew's victory had opened the door to a "sure thing." Pride had invaded my spirit. Instead of desiring to show Christ's love to those to whom He sent me to minister, I only revealed my knowledge of the Scriptures. I was deceived into believing that if I could teach someone to say the correct things and believe the correct way, then they would always have their prayers answered. I now knew that wasn't so.

I'm not underestimating the need for believers to understand who they are in Christ and what their covenant rights are according to the Word. The teaching I received on confessing the Word has been a valuable weapon for changing my life. Please don't think I'm being critical of the wonderful teaching on faith. After Nicolas died in my arms, however, I knew that God was leading me to a deeper place in Him.

For three months following that life changing ordeal of walking in the valley of the shadow of death, I pleaded with the Holy Spirit to teach me His ways:

"Show me Your ways, O LORD; Teach me Your paths. Lead me in Your truth and teach me" (Psalms 25:4-5a).

During this time, the Holy Spirit led me to read *Good Morning, Holy Spirit* by Benny Hinn. My walk with the Lord would never be the same. I began to understand the working of my heavenly companion. I cried out to the Holy Spirit to reveal Himself to me. A stronger relationship with God had begun in my life. For the first time I was experiencing the anointing of God during my prayer time. The Holy Spirit was teaching me to trust Him. He was the one to order my steps. He was the one to bring to my mind the implanted Word for my particular situation. I was sensing a new power in my life.

At the same time, the Holy Spirit was changing my heart. He was teaching me to minister with compassion instead of knowledge. Though knowledge of the Word is fundamental to effective ministry, God's power comes forth when we walk in the love of Christ. The anointing intensifies as we spend time in the presence of God. As my time in His presence increased, the Spirit also convicted me of my fleshly attitudes.

The Lord began to instruct me on the meaning of trust. He encouraged me in my prayer time to put my emotions under the control of my spirit. Since the Holy Spirit is in charge of changing us into the likeness of Christ, I would only need to recognize what He wanted to change and ask Him to do the work. Instead of my soul, it was increasingly the Holy Spirit leading my actions. I was beginning to understand what it meant when Jesus said that He did only what He saw His Father do:

> Most assuredly, I say to you, the Son
> can do nothing of Himself, but what He sees
> the Father do; for whatever He does, the Son
> also does in like manner.
>
> For the Father loves the Son, and shows
> Him all things that He Himself does; and
> He will show Him greater works than these,
> that you may marvel.
>
> John 5:19-20

The relationship of love between the Father and the Son was the source of Jesus' revelation of what the Father was doing. The Father's commands will always line up with His written Word because Jesus is the Word made flesh (John 1:14). In my own life, I need to have a relationship with the Father just as Jesus did. I need to love the Father in the same way so that the Holy Spirit will show me my Father's desire for a situation. Remember, because Jesus is the author and finisher of our faith (Hebrews 12:2), He knows the level of our faith.

What is faith? The Bible says:

> Now faith is the substance of things
> hoped for, the evidence of things not seen.
>
> Hebrews 11:1

Faith is an actual substance in the spirit realm—so either it's there or it's not. Because we live in our mortal bodies, we must rely on the Spirit of God to decide our actions. He knows what faith I have obtained through my walk with Him. He knows

14

how to increase my level of faith for the trials ahead. However, I must be willing to be lead. The direction the Holy Spirit is leading me in must not be hindered by tradition, doubt, or fear. He knows exactly what I need to advance in the ways of God—the books I need to read, the church I need to attend, the Bible study I need to participate in, and the teachers I need to hear.

The Holy Spirit needs to be in charge of your spiritual life so that He can affect every aspect of your natural life. You must be on guard, however, for the enemy of your soul—he would love to keep you trusting in man-made traditions and doctrines. Satan wants you to be dependent on "step-by-step" plans to victory, instead of allowing God to direct you in your particular situation.

Remember that no matter how difficult your situation seems to be:

> God is faithful, who will not allow you to be tempted beyond what you are able, but with the temptation will also make the way of escape, that you may be able to bear it.
>
> 1 Corinthians 10:13

God is your way of escape! You can have victory in every situation if you allow the Holy Spirit to lead you. Don't wait until the trial has overtaken you before seeking guidance from the Holy Spirit. He wants to prepare you now. He prepared my sister for her trial several months before the crisis hit. Many people refuse that small voice of the Spirit until it is too late, then they blame God as if He missed it. But the Scripture says, "If we are faithless, He remains faithful; He cannot deny Himself" (2 Timothy 2:13).

My hunger for the Word of God increased. Little did I know that the Holy Spirit was preparing me for the rapidly approaching attack on my family. During the months immediately following Nicolas's death, I grew in my understanding of God and His love. The desire in my heart to minister to others increased until it became an all consuming passion. Although I was teaching a small Bible study, I knew that God had placed a burden in me to touch thousands with His love.

One night when the intensity of the presence of the Spirit of God was upon me, I cried out from my spirit, "God release me into ministry or take me home." I couldn't stand to live without fulfilling the vision to minister that burned in my soul. Ten days later, the Lord revealed to me that my prayer had reached heaven and that the hedge of protection surrounding my family had been let down so that Satan could test me (see the Book of Job, chapters 1 and 2).

When I first began teaching the Bible, Satan told me that he would kill my daughter. Not understanding my covenant right to protection, I had declared to God that I would serve Him no matter what the cost. Satan was about to test that commitment.

3

The Trap is Set

How was God going to begin the ministry He had placed in my heart? Taking care of my three children, ages two, five, and seven, consumed most of my time. Besides caring for my family, I taught a weekly Bible study and ran a part-time fund raising business. Though I knew that the Lord was calling me to a commitment to minister full-time, I could not imagine how this could happen. With all the activity in my life, my mind had all but forgotten the prayer of desperation uttered to the Lord a week before.

It was now May 22, 1992, and I was focusing on the upcoming Memorial Day weekend. The weekend was to be a preview of the summer vacation that our seven-year-old daughter and her five-year-old and two-year-old brothers were already planning. Little did my husband, John, and I know that other plans were already in progress—plans that the evil one had for the destruction of our family. But God in His wisdom would use those same plans to change the course of our lives.

We were eagerly anticipating the long weekend ahead as we piled into the van and headed for our favorite ice cream parlor. This Friday evening, Williamsburg, Virginia, was full of the hustle and bustle of tourists arriving for the holiday. After the kids finished their ice cream, they convinced their dad and me to take them for a stroll around Williamsburg's restored historical area. Lauren pushed her two-year-old brother along in his stroller. Mitchell was holding his dad's hand and smiling—never before had we strolled along Colonial Williamsburg this late in the evening. We will forever remember that special time together as a family.

Our Saturday morning began with the sound of Lauren's loud giggle. She had opened her bedroom door and seen Michael, her pride and joy, sitting on the potty in the bathroom across the hall from her room. Michael was still too young to worry about closing the bathroom door.

"Look Mom, Michael used the potty," Lauren exclaimed, and then said to her brother, "you're not a baby any more Michael! You're so big!" She was awestruck with her youngest brother's process of growing up.

My husband is an engineer by trade, but John's real passion is flying. He's a part-time flight instructor at a nearby military base, which provides many opportunities for him to fulfill this passion. Saturday mornings normally begin with John instructing a few students before joining the rest of his family in whatever we're doing that day. This Saturday morning, however, he had postponed giving a flying lesson until later in the day because Mitchell had a Tee-ball game. At the age of five, Mitchell was very sports-minded and could not wait to play Tee-ball. He and his father went on to the game before the rest of us.

It was doubtful that Lauren, Michael, and I would arrive in time for the beginning of the game because Lauren's room was a real mess. The rules of the house stated that Lauren had to clean her room before she could go out on Saturday. After Lauren complained about having to clean, we compromised and I helped with the job. She appreciated my help and we had the room cleaned in no time. Finally, we could leave for the big Tee-ball game. As always, Lauren dressed her baby brother, Michael, and had him ready to go in just minutes. She loved mothering her brother and always talked about having babies one day.

On the way to the game we decided to grab lunch at the local drive-through. We arrived at the game in time for the last inning. Lauren clutched her bag of fries and soft drink as she headed for the bleachers. As she placed the fries one by one, almost methodically, into her mouth, John watched her intently. For some unexplainable reason he felt drawn to capture his daughter's image permanently in his mind.

Mitchell's team lost their game, though officially no one was keeping score. After the game, Lauren saw one of her best friends and she went to say hello. Little did her friend realize that when Lauren waved good-bye, they would not share the summer together. For Lauren, the farewell to her friend would be her final good-bye.

As we were leaving the playing field, John told me how much he had enjoyed spending the morning with us and how he regretted the flying lesson he had scheduled for the remainder of the afternoon. He was hoping that the plane he had booked for the afternoon flight was still in the repair shop and that the flying lesson would be canceled.

John went ahead in his car to check on the plane and get ready in the event he had to go to the airport after all. The children rode home with me. During the ride we talked about how we would spend the rest of the day. We discussed going to the beach, but I didn't really want to try to take three small children to the beach on Memorial Day weekend—the busiest weekend of the season. Nevertheless, I told the kids that we could go if their Dad wasn't flying. By the time we got home, however, Mitchell had already decided that he didn't feel like going to the beach. So before checking with John about *his* afternoon plans, we unanimously decided to take advantage of the warm temperature and set up the wading pool on the side lawn. I hoped that John would share in our enthusiasm because he disliked the way the pool always messed up the lawn.

Just as we got out of the car, John came to the front door with the news that the flight was on. We told him of our plans to stay home and use the wading pool. Though in a hurry, he did the unusual and helped us assemble the pool. His action would be of great comfort to me, for later Satan could not accuse me of disregarding

20

my husband's wishes and thereby causing my daughter's accident. I believe wives should submit to their husbands in keeping with Paul's admonition in Ephesians 5:22. Yet if my husband had asked us not to use the pool on the side lawn on that particular weekend, I'm not sure I would have listened. Satan then could have brought guilt and blame into my heart. Although Romans 8:1 states there is no condemnation to those who are in Christ Jesus, I'm thankful I didn't have to battle false accusations.

The children waved good-bye to their dad and excitedly jumped into the wading pool. I changed into my bathing suit and settled into my beach chair to read and get a bit of sun.

After the kids had been in the pool for about thirty minutes, I had them get out for some ice cold lemonade. Lauren, who was always careful not to get hurt, moved all the sticks and rocks from a spot on the lawn about twenty feet from the base of a large tree in our side yard. She loved being close to me, so she picked a spot just to the side and slightly to the rear of my chair to lay out her brand new beach towel. Mitchell could never keep still, so he was busy doing different things. Michael sat on the towel with Lauren. To anyone passing by, we probably looked like the ideal family spending a perfect, sunny day at home.

Once, when I turned and looked at Lauren, I saw her hugging and kissing her two-year-old brother. She truly adored Michael—the same way she adored Mitchell when he was a baby.

21

Meanwhile, Mitchell turned on the tape player and started listening to a music tape by the Christian musician, Carman. Lauren's favorite Christian singer was Twila Paris, so she paid little attention to the music. When Michael heard the music, however, he jumped up from Lauren's towel and ran over to the cassette player. He wanted to join his big brother who was now dancing to the tape. Mitchell's action of playing the tape recorder probably saved Michael's life. It was at that moment that I again felt the evil presence of death near us.

Just two nights before, I had felt that same presence as a drunk driver barely missed hitting my two boys. At that time we were talking to a neighbor who lives on our quiet street, which is more like a country road, since it doesn't have sidewalks or curbs. Without warning, a drunk driver's car sped directly toward the boys who were standing close to the road. When I saw it, I immediately began praying in the Spirit (see 1 Corinthians 14:14-15). The car missed Mitchell and Michael by just a few feet. I reported the incident to the police, forgave the driver, and started praying for his salvation.

Now two days later and without warning, I felt that same spirit of death in our front yard.

4

Death Strikes

Before I could even rebuke the evil presence or lift up a prayer, I heard a loud cracking sound that was followed *immediately* by a horrendous crashing noise next to my chair. As I jumped from my chair, I could see the boys in front of me so I knew they were all right, and since Lauren hadn't cried out I was fairly certain she was also okay. But just as I started to turn to look at her, the Holy Spirit said to me, "I have begun your ministry." Somehow I knew He wouldn't be telling me that if she wasn't hurt.

Lauren had been lying on her stomach with her head propped up in her hands so she could watch her brothers. Now her face was buried into her towel and there was a huge tree limb next to her and a gaping wound in her head where the limb had struck her. A large section of her skull lay next to her and blood was pouring out of the wound. I instantly covered her with as much of her towel as I could while I yelled, "Help, help, call 911!"

Almost unbelievably, in the midst of this surrealistic nightmare, my heart was filled with peace. It was a peace so strong that I wasn't afraid for my daughter's life. I knew somehow that God was with me, and I believed that if it was necessary He would raise Lauren from the dead. He had resurrected my sister's baby just three years before. In the midst of what I was seeing and doing, I truly believed that the supernatural peace I was experiencing meant that God was going to give me a great miracle.

In response to my yell, Mitchell ran inside the house and dialed 911. Then he came back out screaming and crying while holding the telephone. It seems the 911 dispatcher couldn't understand him, but she kept him on the line until someone else called, and then she switched to the other call. That one came from our neighbor's son, Chris Jones, who had heard my cry for help and dialed 911 also. He was now standing outside his house holding a cordless phone while he talked to the dispatcher.

His father, Ron, ran over to help me. I could tell by his face that he knew Lauren was dead. His past experience as a state trooper had exposed him to many tragedies. He stood next to Lauren's body while I ran into the house. Mitchell was crying almost hysterically, not understanding what had happened to his sister and thinking that he had done something wrong that caused the 911 dispatcher to hang up. I told him he had done just the right thing and said, "Mitchell, pray baby, pray, and Jesus will take care of Lauren." He immediately calmed down as he started praying.

My first thought was to call someone who could agree with me for a miracle. I knew that I needed someone who could believe for my daughter's life. My sister Donna came to mind. The Lord had miraculously healed her infant son, Andrew. I dialed her mother-in-law's number in Maryland where she was spending the weekend. Someone answered and told me that Donna was at the mall. I didn't tell them about Lauren, because I only wanted to talk with my sister. I needed to pray with someone who understood the spiritual law of agreement.

I thought next of Fran Mayes, a woman who trusts in the Lord and has been used mightily in my life. Even before I dialed her number, however, I knew she wouldn't answer. The Holy Spirit was placing an assurance in my heart that He was in complete control of the situation. But for some unknown reason He wasn't going to permit the prayer of agreement to take place. In Matthew 18:19, Jesus states: "I say to you that if two of you agree on earth concerning anything they ask, it will be done for them by My Father in heaven." But, though I didn't know why, I knew the Holy Spirit wasn't going to allow me to join my faith with someone who could believe with me.

I then called my husband at the flying club. A friend of his answered and said John was still in the air. As calmly as I could, I told him to radio John and have him come home at once. If my husband was still flying, I didn't want him to panic. At the same time, I didn't want him to take his time coming home. I made certain that John's friend understood that there was an urgent situation. He did, and John was immediately instructed to get home.

After hanging up the receiver, I hurried back to my daughter's side. I realized that I had not taken her pulse. As I started to remove the towel from Lauren and turn her body over to check the pulse at her neck artery, a strong pressure held my hands down. The Holy Spirit stopped me from looking at Lauren's face, which had been disfigured by the force of the limb's impact. In my heart, He whispered for me to leave her covered and not look. This was now just a broken clay vessel—it was not my Lauren.

The message saturated my spirit. Lauren wasn't here anymore. But I was still believing for the Lord to bring her spirit and soul back into this vessel. I lifted her as she lay face down and held her bloody and lifeless body in my arms. I understood then the reason the Lord had been teaching me to place my emotions under the control of my spirit. If I had responded with my emotions, I would have lost all ability to be led by the Holy Spirit. Hysterics would have over-whelmed me if I hadn't learned to trust the Lord. I praise the Lord that His presence was so real. The Holy Spirit supernaturally turned what should have been the worst experience of my life into a time of indescribable peace. It truly was "the peace of God, which surpasses all understanding" (Philippians 4:7).

About that time, Chris ran over and asked if I needed anything. I suddenly realized that I was still in my bathing suit. I didn't want to face a yard full of strangers that way, so I asked Chris to run upstairs and bring me a tee shirt. As I was putting it on, I heard the sirens of the rescue vehicles as they came up our street.

Waving my arms frantically, I ran to the street to make certain they didn't pass by my house. As they hurried out of their vehicles, I shouted at them to have a helicopter waiting. I knew that the seriousness of my daughter's injury could not be treated at our small hospital. Once the rescue workers saw my daughter's lifeless body, however, they didn't attempt to move her. One look and they knew they couldn't help her. Lauren was not in my yard. Lauren was in the arms of Jesus (2 Corinthians 5:1).

The fire chief escorted me into my house and asked me about the accident. There was no logical explanation for the large tree limb breaking off or falling the way it did. Somehow, on a perfectly still day, a 70-pound, 15-foot limb snapped off two inches from the trunk and landed on the opposite side of the tree from where it should have logically fallen. Besides that, the limb was still green inside—there was no sign of any dryness or deadness in it. It was as if some unknown force had torn the live limb from the tree and hurled it like a spear directly toward Lauren. (For further details, see the newspaper article at the end of this chapter.)

The rescue workers talked to me for a while and saw that I wasn't in need of medical assistance. My mind and thoughts kept returning to the Lord. He had not instructed me what to do.

The others may have felt that the situation was hopeless, but I knew the power of God. I told the fireman that I needed to go to my closet. He looked concerned about my unusual request and asked a neighbor to keep an eye on me. I explained to him that I had to pray, and my closet was a prayer closet.

Many times the Lord had revealed His will to me in my prayer closet. I expected to hear from Him this time. If my daughter was to be raised from the dead, the Holy Spirit would need to empower me with faith. He did not answer me, however, even though the peace of God was strong in my heart. How desperately I longed to hear that small voice of God. Despite the natural circumstances, in my mind the fate of Lauren hadn't been decided. I had yet to hear from heaven. I was eagerly awaiting the instructions of the Holy Spirit—but He didn't speak to me. Still wrapped in an indescribable peace, I left my prayer closet

Downstairs the fire chief was waiting to talk with me. He explained that Lauren would not be going to the hospital. Though he couldn't officially tell me that my daughter was dead—only a coroner could make such a declaration—he informed me that his men couldn't do anything for her. At this point, I told him I wanted to go to Lauren to pray for her. He hesitated about letting me—I believe it went against procedure. But I was determined to pray over my baby. God *had* to speak to me. I *had* to know what He wanted me to do (Psalms 37:23-24).

In no uncertain terms, I informed the fire chief that no one could prevent me from praying over my daughter, even though I knew he was only trying to keep me from experiencing what he considered would be additional trauma. After convincing him that the Lord was my strength, we walked out to the yard where Lauren's body lay covered by her beach towel.

As we got close to her, I noticed an object beside the wading pool about three-feet from her body—it was her completely intact brain. The shock of seeing that and suddenly realizing the hopelessness of her situation made me cry out to God. I did not have the faith to put her brain back into her skull and then believe God to heal it. God would have to give me a mighty supernatural gift of faith to believe for such an awesome miracle. I knew that with God nothing is impossible—but still . . .

Lauren was still laying face down, and as I gently placed my hands on her little back my prayer language poured from my lips. Human words would have failed me during such an intense moment. I had to have the perfect will of the Father. Even as I prayed with my spirit, with my mind I pleaded with the Holy Spirit to return life to my daughter's body. I felt that if they found a heartbeat, even if only the brain stem remained intact, the rescue workers would have to take Lauren to a hospital. No matter how long it would take, no matter how impossible it seemed, I would stand by my daughter's hospital bed and believe God for a miracle. God, I reasoned, is able to do anything. I pleaded with Him, "Lord, I am in covenant with you and every night I prayed the blood of Jesus over this child. You must put a heartbeat into her limp body."

Instantly the Lord revealed to my heart that I was asking Him to hook my daughter up to life-support machines for a long time. As if in a daydream I saw Lauren's lifeless body connected to a multitude of machines. During this inner vision I saw my husband growing old and bitter. My boys were not in the vision, and it was as if I would lose them if I insisted God do this my way. I could see myself spending the rest of my life pleading with God to increase my faith to a level where I could believe for the creation of a new brain for Lauren.

Just as the inner vision ended, the voice I had desperately longed to hear spoke gently to my heart: "Daughter, give Lauren to Me." Very simply, very quietly, my wonderful Jesus asked me to trust Him.

During the previous seven years, I had learned to trust that small, still voice. In all things I had learned to obey Him. The Holy Spirit had taken me into a deeper walk with the Lord. He had taught me the power of confessing with my mouth what I believed. As Paul wrote, "And since we have the same spirit of faith, according to what is written, 'I believed and therefore I spoke,' we also believe and therefore speak" (2 Corinthians 4:13). I knew, therefore, that if I verbally told God that Lauren could stay with Him, then God would not raise her from the dead no matter how much I wanted her back.

Weighing the choice that I felt was before me, I knew I had to obey the Lord and trust Him. Still, I cried as I said the words, "Lord, take her—she belongs with You."

No sooner had the words left my mouth than the supernatural presence of God overwhelmed me. I felt as if I were literally inside God and observing this event from heaven's perspective. The Scriptures about abiding in Christ instantly took on deeper meaning. The Holy Spirit completely took over my actions. In my heart I knew that God was beginning a new work in me.

At that moment my husband walked over to me. John had just been told what had happened and that Lauren was dead. He was numb with grief and he cried out to the Lord for help. The rescue workers persuaded him not to look at his little girl. We wrapped our arms tightly around each other and walked into the house.

I had left a message on my mother's answering machine just minutes after Lauren's accident. I thought I would need her to watch the boys while I went to the hospital with Lauren. My mother, Shirley Pearce (now Shirley Burch), knew when she heard the message that something was drastically wrong. She rushed the thirty-minute drive to our house. During the drive the Holy Spirit prepared her for the worse. My mom was a tower of strength by the time she arrived. She immediately called other family members and friends.

An hour had passed since the tree limb had hurtled to the ground. One by one, my family arrived. During this time, the rescue team tried to track down the coroner. For a still unknown reason, it took three hours to get the official statement that our daughter, Lauren Elizabeth Foster, was dead. Many of my neighbors and friends were irate that the county took so long to remove our daughter's body from the yard. I knew, however, that the Holy Spirit was performing a work in the hearts of the rescue crew as they helplessly watched over our daughter's body.

Finally the people from the funeral home came and removed our daughter's body. Five emotionally exhausted rescue workers entered our house and offered their sincere condolences. Those hours of looking at that empty clay vessel had broken their hearts. Out of compassion for me, they asked if there was anything they could do. I thanked them and shook their hands and made them promise to go to a church that truly believes that a personal relationship with Jesus is possible. I encouraged them to find a church that believes and teaches the Word of God—a church where they could find the One who at that moment was bringing me unfathomable peace!

And not only me—peace flooded my mom's spirit also as she heard my request. She knew that the same Jesus that was strengthening her was pouring His grace upon her daughter (2 Corinthians 12:9; Philippians 4:13).

On his way out of the door, a rescue worker handed me Lauren's shorts. She had removed them from over her bathing suit just before entering the pool. I clutched them to my chest and hurried upstairs. For some reason, I wanted to hide them in my closet to keep them forever. They still smelled like my daughter. As I was tucking them into a hiding place, the Holy Spirit instructed me to put them into the washing machine. The Lord was not going to allow me to idolize material objects. He is the source of all comfort and anything else would be a counterfeit. As I put the shorts into the washing machine in the playroom at the end of the upstairs hall, I realized that God was teaching me His way to grieve—a way of peace, comfort, and healing.

By this time our pastor had arrived and was sitting at the kitchen table. I recalled the conversation we had had months earlier after Nicolas had died. At that time, my pastor confided in me that the worst duty of his position was performing funerals for children. As he sat at my table, with Lauren's sudden death still hard to grasp, I thought he was praying for guidance to perform that dreaded duty. Later he told me he sat in our kitchen in a state of awe over the grace of God that he saw us experiencing.

By seven-thirty that evening, only the immediate family remained at our home. My sister Donna had just arrived with her family. We had walked through trials before, but this one would test our fundamental trust in God's Word.

During her drive from Maryland, Donna had asked God, "Lord, You *are* going to raise Lauren from the dead, aren't You?" The thought would not leave her. She knew that God was a good God. She lived daily with the reality of the miracle working power of God. Her son is a walking and breathing miracle. Medically speaking, Andrew should never have breathed or walked on his own. However, he was a very active child that could even run without the assistance of a breathing machine, and he was growing stronger every day. Where was the God who raised Andrew from death?

In answer to Donna's question, the Lord gave her an inner vision: She saw angels pulling Lauren from her body just seconds before the tree limb struck her. When Donna told me that, I realized that that was the reason why Lauren hadn't cried out in pain as the limb hit her. Donna said the Holy Spirit also told her that she had to believe in a different way this time than she had for Andrew.

Some time later I asked Mitchell what he had last seen of Lauren—he had been watching her just before the limb fell and I wanted to know his last impressions of her. Mitchell told me that Lauren had been lying on her stomach with her head propped up on her arms, watching him and Michael. He said that just before the limb struck her, Lauren suddenly fell face forward onto her towel and didn't move again. This confirmed the truth of Donna's inner vision.

By 11:00 p.m. the last of our house guests had left. Michael and Mitchell were in bed. As we tucked them in, John and I wondered if they understood what had happened and if they were emotionally okay. We prayed over them before we went into our bedroom.

Alone in our room, we held each other and sobbed. The pain of our sorrow and grief tore through us and almost overwhelmed us. It felt as if our very hearts had been cut out. Trying to lessen our pain, we left our room and went into Lauren's bedroom. But that just made it worse. As we stood there in that empty room that would never again echo with the loud giggle of our beloved Lauren, we cried aloud in anguish. What would we do without our daughter—what would Michael and Mitchell do without their sister?

Suddenly Mitchell yelled at us to quit crying— that he couldn't sleep with all the noise we were making.

At the sound of Mitchell's voice and child-concern for his sleep, John and I knew that our family life would somehow go on and our pain would heal.

God was watching over us, and everything would be all right.

Grieving parents consoled
Friends remember girl's faith, strength
By Leslie Postal - *Daily Press*

YORK

Other children in the church group had struggled over the assignment, not sure what to write to the missionaries overseas. But seven-year-old Lauren Elizabeth Foster had known just what she wanted to say.

From memory she wrote, "Though I walk through the valley of the shadow of death I will fear no evil. For you are with me. Your rod and your staff they comfort me."

Her parents held the letter close Sunday as they mourned their young daughter's death. She died Saturday in what her father, John Foster, called the "freakiest of freak accidents."

That afternoon, Lauren was in the side yard of the family's Country Club Acres home, just outside Williamsburg. She was playing with her two brothers in the wading pool her parents had just cleaned and repaired. About 2 p.m., she spread out her towel and lay down.

A few minutes later, a limb from one of the tall trees that ring the Foster's yard fell on her, crushing her skull and killing her instantly. The York County Sheriff's Department said the 15-foot limb weighed at least 75 pounds and fell about 40 feet. Police did not know why it came down.

"All the trees in the yard are going to be cut down," John Foster said.

There is some comfort in that Lauren died so quickly, without much suffering, said her mother, Cyndi. And much more in reading the letter and remembering "she loved the Lord."

Lauren wrote the letter last Monday, but it hadn't been mailed yet when she died. Greensprings Chapel in Williamsburg, the family's church, returned it to her parents.

"It was just so strange for a seven-year-old to write that," said Cyndi Foster. "That's someone who knew Jesus," she said.

The Fosters sat surrounded by family and friends Sunday.

"The neighborhood has been wonderful. It's been like a church," Cyndi Foster said. "People we don't know have been bringing food over."

Lauren was just about to finish the second grade at Williamsburg Christian Academy, which she had attended since she was four.

"She was such a sweet little girl," said Katie Haas, the school's secretary. "And she was an excellent student," Haas said, "just a real example to other kids."

Lauren loved her dolls, the color pink and to write skits, her parents said. And she and her cousin, Casey, loved to pretend they were sisters.

She doted over her younger brothers, Michael, 2, and Mitchell, 5, teaching them the ABCs and even changing their diapers when they were younger.

"The five-year-old knows she's gone. He doesn't really understand death, but he knows she's in heaven," John Foster said.

"The little one, he's just been running around looking for her," his wife added.

The death was a shock for many at the school, Haas said. The academy plans to start an annual award and a missionary fund in Lauren's name, she added.

"[For] Lauren, as little as she was, that was her main life's goal, the missionaries. She loved the missionaries," Haas said.

Her parents said they find solace in remembering that.

"Knowing how strong she was has given us strength, too," said John Foster, who works for the flight applications division of NASA. "She touched a lot of people. She was special."

5

Sufficient Grace

At two o'clock Sunday morning, I awoke and realized that the accident was not just a dream. My Lauren was not in her room with her dolls and stuffed animals. My Lauren was with the Lord. Needing to be close to God, I went to my prayer closet.

As I prayed I found myself thanking the Lord that Lauren wasn't suffering. As I thanked the Lord, the sorrow and grief that had overwhelmed me hours earlier fled. The grace of God would see me through this trial. I completely surrendered my life into the hands of our all-knowing God as I realized He was doing something so great in me that I couldn't comprehend it. I did nothing but worship Him for over an hour.

Daylight came with the telephone ringing almost continuously. The news about Lauren had spread quickly. Our family and friends started arriving at the house. The company of so many caring people helped us get through our first day without Lauren.

Though it didn't make sense, I called my sister-in-law and asked her if she would cut my hair. She owned a beauty parlor and was willing to help me in any way possible. My two sisters met us there. They were so considerate to let me talk about the previous day's event. I just had to talk about the accident. As difficult as it was for me to share the details, I knew it was more difficult to hear them. Nevertheless, it helped me come to terms with what happened.

Once we returned to my home, I spent the day telling anyone who would listen about the circumstances surrounding Lauren's death. Many people called to say that they were praying for us. Their prayers brought strength into our situation. It was now Sunday morning, and in pulpits across our town pastors asked their congregations to pray for us.

A reporter called from the local newspaper and wanted to come over to pick up a photo to run with the news story about the accident. John and I looked forward to meeting with her. When she arrived we spoke with her about our faith in Jesus Christ. She wrote a wonderful article about our daughter and her love for God. It was exciting to see an article glorifying God on the front page of our local paper. God was already bringing forth fruit from the seed that fell to the ground (see John 12:24).

One of the most difficult tasks for me was picking out a casket and arranging the burial details. The reality that our body is but dust pierces the soul when you look mortality in the face. As we sat in a small room in the funeral home making decisions about the upcoming services, the truth hit me with full impact—Lauren was with Jesus, and He is all that matters in this life. I would serve Him with all my heart, all my soul, and all my strength. God's grace was sufficient as we chose the casket that would one day break open and release Lauren's body—and thereby release that body to be reunited with her soul and spirit (see 1 Thessalonians 4:14-17).

After the funeral arrangements were made, John and I went to talk with our pastor about the memorial service. We didn't want anyone to think that the Lord had caused our daughter to die at the age of seven. Jesus was holding us up and I could not stand to hear anyone blame Him for what the enemy had done. Lauren's accident was not an act of love from the Lord; it was an attempt from Satan to destroy our family and the ministry that God was calling us to (see John 10:10).

When we spoke with our pastor, I told him that the Lord had told me that I was to share at the funeral service. He agreed to our request. He said that if I still felt like speaking on the morning of the funeral, then he would give me time. Though I had no idea what I would say, I knew that I was obeying the Holy Spirit with my request.

Monday morning came and it was time for the immediate family to meet at the funeral home for the viewing. I dreaded seeing my little girl in that casket. As John and I entered the room, we realized what a beautiful daughter the Lord had blessed us with. We were pleased to see the work done to restore the damage done to her head by the tree limb. It was comforting seeing our daughter's face one last time on this side of eternity.

The Holy Spirit had me share with John the secret I had learned of how to release our loved one's spirit to the Lord and be set free from grief. I believe that the grace for healing begins when we openly declare to the Lord that we freely release our loved one—or whatever the cause of our grief—into His care. In the Scriptures, both Jesus (Luke 23:46) and Stephen (Acts 7:59) release their spirits unto the Father. I believe that as a parent I have authority over my children's spirits while they are alive—that's why the Holy Spirit taught me this truth. The letting go of our grief and sorrow for our loved one is an act of faith and trust. Such faith pleases God, and we are now able to receive the grace we need for the healing of our grief and sorrow.

As John knelt down at his daughter's casket, I felt the atmosphere in the room change. Later, he told me that he had released her to the Lord during that special moment. When he did, he was filled with a new strength.

Meanwhile, the rest of the family entered the room for what was supposed to be their final look at Lauren's vessel. John and I decided to have the casket closed during the evening viewing and at the funeral service, even though my father and his wife, Lewis and Nancy Pearce, had asked us to leave the casket open during the viewing. At the time, we felt that it would be too sad for others to see the lifeless body of such a young child. After we made our request known to the funeral director, however, the Holy Spirit began tugging at John's heart. He called me to the side and said he needed to talk with me alone. Together we found an empty prayer room. He explained that logically he felt we were making the right decision, but in his heart he felt uneasy about it.

After prayer, the Holy Spirit revealed to me that the newspaper's graphic description of the accident had left many with a picture of Lauren's destroyed face. The Lord wanted to replace that image with one of beauty. The people needed to look at Lauren's lovely face one last time. Now I understood that the Lord desired to heal everyone who would come to pay their respects to our family.

My father was delighted when we told him we were going to leave the casket open for the viewing. We wanted the funeral service to be a celebration of life, however, so we decided to keep the casket closed during the service the next morning. The focus of the ceremony would be on Lauren's eternal home with Jesus.

The next few hours flew by as out-of-town family visitors began arriving. The telephone rang nonstop with people calling us. Our neighbors, the families from Lauren's school, and our church were working overtime to ease our burden. When six o'clock arrived, we headed for our last look at our daughter's beautiful vessel.

The general public began arriving at seven. Hundreds of people went through the receiving line to offer their condolences. The power of God was mightily upon me. One by one, I hugged and encouraged them with the strength God was giving me. They could not understand the peace and joy that God had placed in my heart—it was beyond their understanding, and beyond mine (see Philippians 4:7).

The Holy Spirit gave me individual words of comfort to reassure the friends, family, and co-workers that surrounded us for two hours. The loving response of so many people who truly hurt for us was overwhelming. As each person approached me, I felt the Spirit lift me up. As I ministered to these people by the power of God, more healing took place in my own heart (see Philippians 4:7).

As the last visitors talked to me, the anointing of the Holy Spirit was tremendous. I was overcome with joy. Not wanting anyone to think I was medicated or drunk, I asked the Lord to tone it down a little. It was so strong I was almost drunk on the new wine of the Holy Spirit (see Acts 2:15-16). Jesus alone deserves the credit for getting me through this tragic time!

After the last visitor left, the funeral director told us to take our time saying good-bye to our daughter. He knew that when we closed the casket lid for the last time, it would be the end of our family life as we had known it.

As we looked at the lovely vessel that had contained our daughter, John took my hand and I prayed: "Father, thank You that Lauren had such a beautiful vessel while she was here with us. She is the handiwork of a loving Lord. Jesus, thank You that she isn't here suffering. She is where she can never be harmed again. Lord, praise You that we will all be together soon. Amen."

Hand in hand we walked out of the funeral home. The peace of God filled my heart.

I looked up at the stars and thanked God again for the unbelievable joy I was experiencing.

6

The Vision

When I went to bed later that night, I slept soundly until about 2 a.m., and then couldn't sleep any longer—so I went downstairs to pray. My Walkman™ cassette player was on the kitchen counter. As I placed the earphones over my ears and pushed the start button, a strange sensation poured through me. The music from the praise tape sounded as if it was coming from a heavenly orchestra. Quickly I made my way to the sofa in the family room and laid down as the power of God came upon me.

Suddenly I saw with my natural eyes a window appearing on my ceiling. I was completely awake and aware of my surroundings. Seconds later, Lauren appeared in the window. God was letting me see my daughter.

The first thing I noticed was that her hair color had changed. Rather than the brownish gold it was at the time of her death, it was the "pure" golden blond it had been when she was a baby, and it was wavy and flowing instead of straight. Though I couldn't account for the change, I knew that Lauren must have always wanted wavy golden hair and God had given it to her in heaven.

There were no other changes in her appearance except for the glory that was upon her. But she was still my Lauren.

Her face radiated with the newness of eternal life. I could tell that she could see me and was as thrilled as I was to see her. It was wonderful to see my little girl so full of life. With a giggle and the mannerism that belonged only to Lauren, she said, "Thank you, Mommy, for giving me to Jesus." With almost a squeal of delight she added, "Daddy gave me to Jesus, too."

Lauren was in a grassy field and began to dance and dance. There were some people with her and I recognized a few of them. As I saw her joy, and the joy of the others around her, I realized more than ever before that this life offers only a fraction of the joy that awaits every believer in heaven.

"Lord," I whispered, " if anyone dies and goes to be with You, I will not be sad."

Joy and peace filled my soul. Heaven was beyond human expression. If the vision had ended after just a glimpse of my Lauren, I would have received more from the Lord than I had ever expected. My heart was at peace. God was doing more for me than I had ever asked.

But the vision was only beginning.

I saw people dressed in flowing white gowns hurrying toward the grassy field and surrounding my daughter—their rapid movement was so graceful they seemed to be dancing. In the midst of them was the most glorious Person in all creation—it was Jesus, my Lord and Savior. He was looking intently toward me. Love radiated from every part of Him. Truly, I was gazing into the face of perfection. His eyes were like pools of pure love—a love we can only hope to experience in this life, but will know forever in the life to come.

As I watched, the Lord reached down and picked Lauren up in His strong arms. Triumphantly He placed her on one shoulder. It was as if she were a champion that was being paraded about in a victory march. The crowd broke into applause. Shouts of joy and praise filled the atmosphere. Then a silence fell over the people. Lauren looked down into the eyes of her Lord, and I knew then that she belonged to Him. I also knew that there was nothing more sacred and holy than belonging to Jesus.

Just before the vision vanished as quickly as it had appeared, Lauren turned toward me and said again, "Mommy, thank you for giving me to Jesus."

The awesomeness of the experience overwhelmed me. Now I knew what to share during my daughter's funeral service.

My little girl was not in that cold, dark casket sitting in the sanctuary.

She was safe in the arms of Jesus.

7

The Funeral

After the vision, I was able to get a few hours of sleep before the morning funeral service. Joy and peace saturated my spirit, so much so that while making preparations for the service I continually referred to the occasion as a *wedding*. The word *funeral* just seemed inappropriate. In remembrance of Lauren, the immediate family wore pink because she loved that color so much. John, who rarely wears his light pink dress shirt, wore it for his daughter's funeral. We imagine Lauren's neighbors in heaven had been wondering who Jesus was preparing a pink mansion for—either a Mary Kay representative or our dainty Lauren.

During the remaining couple of hours before the service everything seemed chaotic and rushed. Despite the confusion, I felt the strong peace of the Lord. I cannot explain the wonderful grace of the Lord Jesus Christ. I can only hope to encourage you by our family's testimony to "trust in the Lord with all your heart, And lean not on your own understanding" (Proverbs 3:5). On this day that should have been so unbearable, we had peace and strength that was far beyond our own abilities (see Philippians 4:6-7).

After all the family had gathered at our home, the funeral director had them line up their cars in the appropriate order. Finally the time came and we headed toward the church. As we arrived at Greensprings Chapel, we saw cars parked in every available space. The chapel's seating capacity of about 300 was too small to contain the crowd. People lined the hallways. Many unknown faces were in the congregation. It seemed as though all of Williamsburg wanted to pay their respects to Lauren and our family.

Twila Paris's recording of "Sanctuary" had just finished playing as we approached the front of the chapel. Lauren had wanted to be a Christian singer just like her. She had made her own tape by singing Twila Paris songs. The tape Lauren left behind of her singing has brought our family much joy. We imagine her singing for Jesus in heaven has brought her much joy.

The service began with an introduction of our daughter's Christian school principal, Debra Cotorceanu. She spoke of the love the school had for Lauren and how precious our little girl was to her teachers and classmates. The people at the school had such a love in their hearts for our family. We'll never forget their kindness. Not only did they provide emotional support and prayers, but they continued to prepare meals for us for weeks after the funeral when we were still trying to adjust to life without Lauren.

Lauren's teacher from her Missionette's Club was the next to share. Our daughter loved earning badges and learning more about the Lord during her weekly meetings at Missionettes. On the Monday night before Lauren's death, all the girls wrote a letter of encouragement to different missionaries. Lauren's assignment was to write to the Hause family in the Philippines. Her teacher, Ro Seaman, explained that Lauren knew exactly what she wanted to write to her missionary family. She read the card that our daughter had written on that night:

> *God is with you . . . Yes, though I walk through the valley of the shadow of death. I will fear no evil. For you are with me. Your rod and your staff they comfort me.*
>
> *I am 7 year old.*
>
> *Love,*
> *Lauren Foster*

The card, adorned with pink hearts, was never mailed to its Philippine destination. When Ro and her husband, Tim, learned of Lauren's death, the Holy Spirit directed them to give the card to us. The pink hearts touched our hearts. Little did Lauren know that her handiwork would encourage the people she loved most. What a merciful God who would care for us with such a special gift of love!

It was now time for our daughter's dearest friend and neighbor, twelve-year-old Amber Lucento, to sing,

Dear, Mrs. + Mr. Hause

Yes though I walk
through the valley
of the shadow of
death. I will fear no
evil. For you are with me.
Your rod and your staff
they comfort me.

I am 7 year old
Love, Lauren Foster

God is
with
you!

"Lamb of God"—a Twila Paris song she had selected for this occasion. Jane Vaught, Lauren's first grade teacher, began to play the accompaniment. Instead of words ringing through the church, however, only sobs were coming from this precious child. I could not allow her to feel as though she had let us down. I did not want her to leave embarrassed and hurt.

Before I even knew what I was doing, the Holy Spirit had me standing beside Amber. Together we sang one of my daughter's favorite songs of adoration for the Lord. As we finished, a sense of peace fell over the congregation. The Spirit of the Lord was present in an undeniable way. His peace filled the hearts of all who were gathered to mourn our daughter. Amber and I will never forget the bonding that occurred between us as we sang to the Lord. She walked back to her seat with a heart touched by God. Sorrow and grief never overtook Amber again. To this day, we give the Lord all the glory and praise for what He did in her heart.

Pastor Bob Atkins informed those gathered that the Foster's had requested that a video of Lauren reciting a poem be shown. Many people had commented how deeply touched they were by our daughter's performance at the 1991 "Speech Meet" at school. Though it was only a short video, on the screen was the essence of our daughter's life on this earth for all to see—that essence was her obvious love for her Lord Jesus. Her hair flowed in gentle waves from the rollers she had insisted on sleeping in the night before her recitation. She had chosen to wear her blue and white flowered dress. Lauren Elizabeth Foster was on center stage one last time. With a joy for the Lord in her heart that radiated from the very depths of her spirit, she recited this poem:

I Think When I Read That Sweet Story of Old
By Jemima Luke

I think when I read that sweet story of old

When Jesus was here among men,

How He called little children as lambs to His fold,

I should like to have been with them then.

I wish that His hands had been placed on my head,

That His arms had been thrown around me,

And that I might have seen His kind look when He said,

"Let the little ones come unto me."

Following the video, our pastor had planned to deliver a message from the Bible, but he was overwhelmed with emotion and felt that he could not go on. He told me later that when he really thought he could not share his message, he looked over at me. I mouthed to him that he could do it and I smiled. It was enough to encourage him to try. When he did, the grace of God came upon him and he shared beautifully some stories we had told him concerning our daughter. Several people told me afterward that as our pastor spoke of Lauren's love for the Lord, they were convicted of their own lukewarmness concerning the things of God.

Reverend Atkins shared how Lauren had one motivation for wanting to learn to read—she wanted to be able to read her Bible. He told how, as a small child, Lauren would bring her children's picture Bible into my room. As I read my Bible, she would snuggle next to me and pretend to read from hers. Then he recounted the time when she cried after some unsaved friends had left our house. She was upset because I had told them about Jesus before she had a chance. Finally he told how Lauren had given all the money she had saved to the church for the purchase of Bibles for Russia. Because of one little girl's love for missionary work, people were encouraged to support a mission fund established in her honor. More than $1,400 was sent to the mission field because of the "Lauren Elizabeth Foster Mission Fund."

As he finished, our pastor looked over at me to see if I still wanted to share something with the people. I got up and went to the podium. The Lord had placed on my heart to give all glory to Him. Those downcast souls had to be told of the faithfulness of God. I shared the vision the Lord had granted to me just hours before the funeral. The anointing was upon me as I recounted the wonderment of seeing my little girl in the arms of Jesus. I wanted the people to know that Jesus is alive and He is not only interested in us after we die—He wants to abide with us now.

As I shared, my heart went out to the teenagers from Williamsburg Christian Academy who had just returned from a mission trip to Mexico. A tremendous move of God occurred during the trip. Many of these young people received the baptism of the Holy Spirit. (Some received their calling into full-time ministry and are now, at the time I'm writing this, attending seminary.) I didn't want the enemy to use my daughter's death to hinder the work the Lord had begun in their hearts. All of them were downcast about her death, and some of them had even started to blame God for her death and weren't certain they could trust Him anymore.

As we left the church for the forty-five-minute ride to the burial site, I remember watching my boys, Mitchell and Michael, playing in the limousine. Seeing only the boys with their father seemed right to me. God had prepared me since my childhood to raise two boys. Now I was looking at the family I had always thought I would have. It's not that I did not want a daughter, she was the most wonderful surprise of my life, but in my heart God had prepared me to live without a daughter.

Finally we arrived at the cemetery. I don't understand how God's grace carried us through that time. I just know that His grace was more real than the air that we breathe, and it continues to be sufficient to this day.

The pastor led everyone in a salvation prayer at the graveside service. Only the Lord knows how many people entered the Kingdom of God on that warm May day, right there next to Lauren's grave. I pray that many of our unsaved relatives, friends, and co-workers meant the words they prayed after our minister.

If you've never surrendered your life to our Lord Jesus Christ, don't let another minute pass without the assurance that you'll spend eternity in heaven. In the same way that many prayed this prayer at the grave side, you too can receive Jesus Christ. You need only to repent of your sins, turn to God by praying this prayer from your heart, tell others about your conversion, and begin to live a life that demonstrates your faith in Christ:

> Lord Jesus, thank You for suffering on the Cross for me so that I would not have to suffer eternally for my sins. Forgive me of all the sins I have ever committed and be my Lord and Savior now and forever. Come into my heart and cleanse it so I can truly live for You. Thank You, Lord Jesus, for saving me and giving me eternal life. Amen.

Many families from Lauren's school came by our house the next day. A few of her classmates very carefully cleaned my daughter's room, which I didn't know they were doing. When they finished, they called me to come to my daughter's room to see what they had done. Their thoughtfulness brought joy to my heart. In the midst of their hurt and pain, they gave of themselves. As I entered the room filled with shelves of dolls—Lauren always called it her "Doll Shop"—the thought to give something back to these children entered my mind. So I had each of Lauren's friends pick a doll or stuffed animal as a keepsake. It delighted them to have a permanent reminder of their friendship with Lauren.

As I gave back to them, more healing took place in my own heart. During the following week, I went to Lauren's class and gave each of her 14 classmates a doll or stuffed animal—Lauren had over 40 of them. I wanted no one to feel left out.

Two days after the funeral, John's parents, Karl and Maxie Foster, returned to West Virginia. Since their arrival the day after Lauren died, they had waited on *us* hand and foot without concern for their own sorrow. Now they needed to be back to their familiar surroundings where their friends could console *them*.

8

Where Were the Angels?

Just days after the funeral, I had a conversation with a teenager that had baby-sat my daughter. She approached me while I was out in my yard.

"Mrs. Foster, I owe you my life," she cried.

This young lady had been having problems with hearing voices and having thoughts of suicide—she had been receiving psychiatric care for some time. She told me that one day she was thinking of cutting her wrist when she *just happened* to remember a card from me that had arrived in the mail that day. As she picked up the card and read it, she noticed the tract tucked away inside. She read the tract and received Jesus as Lord. The voice in her head stopped and all thoughts of suicide ceased as Jesus came into her heart.

As she told me her story, the girl began to weep. She felt that Lauren's death was her fault. Satan had convinced her that before she was converted she was responsible for bringing the spirit of death into our home when she baby-sat Lauren. I could sense that condemnation was heavy upon her heart. After

61

Lauren's death, she said she stood in the woods behind our home and stared at the spot where our daughter had met her tragic death.

During this time, the Lord in His mercy gave her a vision. She did not understand about spiritual visions, but she knew that what she had called a hallucination brought peace to her soul. While staring intently into our yard, she saw angels pull Lauren from her body before the tree limb hit her. The teen-ager's vision was confirmation that my sister, Donna, had correctly interpreted a message God had given her.

After hearing of the accident, Donna asked the Lord where Lauren's angels were when she was killed. She was told that Lauren was pulled from her body before the tree limb struck her. I know that my little Lauren was with the angels when the limb fell on her body. That's why she didn't cry out in pain when the limb hit her. Satan could only destroy an empty clay vessel!

I comforted this teenager with the truth. Satan was no stranger in my life—we were well-acquainted long before she had begun baby-sitting Lauren. Seven years ago, when I totally dedicated my life to the Lord, the enemy came to me after I had just finished teaching a weekly Bible study. In a voice that was very real, Satan said he would kill my daughter if I continued to teach a Bible study. Knowing very little about spiritual warfare at the time, I went before the Lord and told Him that I would serve Him no matter the cost. The Lord knew I had chosen to serve Him long before the enemy carried through on his threat. The Lord has been faithful to reveal all things to me concerning Lauren's death.

After speaking with this young woman, I walked her home. Her mother had never been healed after the death of a stepson, and the Lord allowed me to minister to her. By exposing the root causes of sorrow and grief, this mother's healing could begin. God was already bringing forth much good from the attack of the enemy. God is awesome! When we receive the truth from His Word, He always turns our tragedies into triumphs. We need not fear, we need only to trust in the One who can do abundantly more than we can ask or think (see Ephesians 3:20-21).

Section Two

Victory for all Believers

L.F.

9

Authority of the Believer

Two weeks after the funeral, a teacher from my daughter's school gave me some pictures Lauren had drawn just before her death. One chalk drawing stood out from the others. To the far right of the page was a black, bird-like creature that resembled a demon. It was fleeing from a huge tree beside a house. I knew instantly that this drawing represented the spirit realm the moment my daughter died.

As I looked at Lauren's strange drawing, my mind raced back to the night before Lauren's accident. I remember her coming downstairs and asking me if I knew that all her relatives would be in heaven one day. I assured her that through prayer all our loved ones would be saved. She cried and told me that she couldn't stand the thought of anyone dying without knowing Jesus. Assured by my answer, she went back to her room.

A half hour later, she came downstairs and asked me what it would be like when she died. Though I thought I was speaking of the rapture, I told her that she would be instantly with the Lord. In the same way that I had unknowingly foretold her death, I knew that the Spirit of God had impressed my daughter to draw the picture I was holding. He wanted me to know that He was not the One who had caused that deadly limb to fall. Satan comes to a believer to destroy their faith in God. He devises schemes of destruction against God's people. The apostle Peter warns us: "Be sober, be vigilant; because your adversary the devil walks about like a roaring lion, seeking whom he may devour (1 Peter 5:8).

Repeatedly over the last four years the Holy Spirit has brought the following verse to my mind: "My lord, O king, let the iniquity be on me and on my father's house, and the king and his throne be guiltless" (2 Samuel 14:9).

Before the accident, I never understood this rhema-word from the Lord. (A rhema-word refers to a specific Scripture that the Holy Spirit gives to a person concerning their need or request.) The meaning became clear, however, with Lauren's death. The Lord did not want me to blame Him for the evil that had occurred. The Holy Spirit used this specific Scripture to declare that we are to blame for allowing the enemy to steal from us. God has given us authority over the works of Satan.

After the Cross, Jesus was given all authority. God the Father declared the name of Jesus to be above all other names:

> And being found in appearance as a man, He humbled Himself and became obedient to the point of death, even the death of the cross.

> Therefore God also has highly exalted Him and given Him the name which is above every name,
>
> that at the name of Jesus every knee should bow, of those in heaven, and of those on earth, and of those under the earth,
>
> and that every tongue should confess that Jesus Christ is Lord, to the glory of the Father.
>
> Philippians 2:8-11

To understand clearly that Jesus has dominion over the enemy, we need to study what Paul declared in Ephesians:

> . . . He [God] raised Him [Jesus] from the dead and seated Him at His right hand in the heavenly places,
>
> far above all principality and power and might and dominion, and every name that is named, not only in this age but also in that which is to come.
>
> And He put all things under His feet, and gave Him to be head over all things to the church,
>
> which is His body, the fullness of Him who fills all in all.
>
> Ephesians 1:20-23

Jesus now has all authority, and He has chosen to make that authority known through His Church, which we are:

And Jesus came and spoke to them, saying, "All authority has been given to Me in heaven and on earth.

"Go therefore and make disciples of all the nations, baptizing them in the name of the Father and of the Son and of the Holy Spirit,

"teaching them to observe all things that I have commanded you; and lo, I am with you always, even to the end of the age." Amen.

Matthew 28:18-20

To do this, He decreed that His followers would have the right to use His name and the power assigned to that name:

Most assuredly, I say to you, he who believes in Me, the works that I do he will do also; and greater works than these he will do, because I go to My Father.

And whatever you ask in My name, that I will do, that the Father may be glorified in the Son.

If you ask anything in My name, I will do it.

John 14:12-14

I chose to believe the Word of God. I knew that God could not be defeated by the devil—even the thought was ludicrous. The Holy Spirit revealed to me that the problem was that the enemy had found *my* weaknesses and used them to attack my faith. I am grateful for a God who can still bring forth victory when we miss His leading. As Christians we need to take seriously our responsibility in the battle that rages with the enemy:

> For we do not wrestle against flesh and blood, but against principalities, against powers, against the rulers of the darkness of this age, against spiritual hosts of wickedness in the heavenly places.
>
> Ephesians 6:12

Clearly Paul is pointing out that the battle we face is between the believer and the powers of Satan. Considering the unseen power of our enemy, it might seem like we would be overwhelmed in such a battle—but we are not helpless in this war, Jesus gave us mighty weapons of warfare:

> Therefore take up the whole armor of God, that you may be able to withstand in the evil day, and having done all, to stand.
>
> Stand therefore, having girded your waist with truth, having put on the breastplate of righteousness,
>
> and having shod your feet with the preparation of the gospel of peace;
>
> above all, taking the shield of faith with which you will be able to quench all the fiery darts of the wicked one.

> And take the helmet of salvation, and the sword of the Spirit, which is the word of God;
>
> praying always with all prayer and supplication in the Spirit, being watchful to this end with all perseverance and supplication for all the saints; . . .
>
> Ephesians 6:13-18

What do I mean by spiritual warfare? I mean praying with your spirit and your understanding against the spiritual forces behind the negative situations, circumstances, and people that affect your life. Ask the Holy Spirit to guide you and teach you in this. Meditate in the Word of God daily (Psalms 1:1-3) and it will change your life for the better. As you grow in your understanding of God's Word, you will also grow in your relationship with God.

Though you may have come through a horrible tragedy that hurt you deeply—or may even be experiencing one now—from this moment on trust the Holy Spirit to bring good out of your situation. Both the Old Testament and the New Testament saints experienced this so many times, that the apostle Paul wrote with full confidence:

> And we know that all things work together for good to those who love God, to those who are the called according to His purpose.
>
> Romans 8:28

Our God is so awesome that whatever Satan has conspired against us, no matter how much victory he seems to have achieved, the minute we turn to God's Word and ask for deliverance, He is faithful to us. And no matter what the situation, remember Paul's admonition: "Do not be overcome by evil, but overcome evil with good" (Romans 12:21).

There are many anointed books and tapes on spiritual warfare, the authority of the believer, the name of Jesus, and the power of the blood. Put away any man-made doctrine that will impede the Holy Spirit's work in you. Ask the Holy Spirit to direct you to the teachers He desires you to hear.

You may feel that you did warfare but God failed you. You may feel like running away from the truth of your authority in Christ. Unfortunately, you may even accept your defeat as God's will. I know how that feels. When that little boy died in my arms, I felt like running, too. However, the Spirit of God would not give me peace when I compromised the truth of God's Word. Instead, He brought me into a greater understanding of His role in my life.

God is perfecting us for the last great battle for souls. We need to quit blaming God for the bad things that happen to us. Furthermore, we must stop interpreting the Word of God according to our failures. We will develop maturity as we accept our responsibility to fight the enemy with our God-given authority. After Lauren died, I repented for allowing the enemy to steal from me. Instead of running from the truth of God's Word, I embraced repentance just as David did:

David perceived that the child was dead. Therefore David said to his servants, "Is the child dead?" And they said, "He is dead."

So David arose from the ground, washed and anointed himself, and changed his clothes; and he went into the house of the Lord and worshiped. Then he went to his own house; and when he requested, they set food before him, and he ate.

Then his servants said to him, "What is this that you have done? You fasted and wept for the child while he was alive, but when the child died, you arose and ate food."

And he said, "While the child was alive, I fasted and wept; for I said 'Who can tell whether the Lord will be gracious to me, that the child may live?'

"But now he is dead; why should I fast? Can I bring him back again? I shall go to him, but he shall not return to me."

Then David comforted Bathsheba his wife.

2 Samuel 12:19-24a

The Holy Spirit used David's example to teach me three truths about winning the battle against sorrow and grief.

First, I had prayed and sought the Lord's will until I knew that He required me to release Lauren's spirit to Him. Every situation is different, Jesus is the author and finisher of your faith (Hebrews 12:2), and God's Spirit will instruct you based on the level of faith you have acquired.

Second, the truth of the Cross and God's redemptive plan was ever so relevant. I knew that Lauren was in heaven and that I would see her again, just as David could worship God because he knew that God would reunite him with his son. I could praise God and thank Him for the message of the Cross (1 Corinthians 1:18). My separation from Lauren is only temporary. I will enjoy my daughter's company throughout eternity.

Third, because I could draw comfort from the promise of a heavenly reunion, I could receive God's grace, which enabled me to comfort my loved ones.

Although David was under God's judgment, the reason for his child's death is not the issue. David's reaction to his son's death is still a good biblical example of how to receive God's grace in a tragic situation.

Before Nicolas's death, I had gained much knowledge from the teachings on faith and healing. However, I did not understand the importance of my relationship with the Holy Spirit. This relationship is fundamental in changing our inner man. We need this internal change to take place as our knowledge increases. One without the other will lead to spiritual pride. It is time for us to embrace increasingly the Holy Spirit and His work of sanctification—that is, for us to be more and more separated unto God for His use. Balance will result as we combine the sanctifying work of God with the deeper understandings that are revealed by the Spirit as we study the Word.

The relationship with the Holy Spirit is the most vital ingredient to walking and living in victory. Now, because of my relationship with the Holy Spirit, I can live in victory instead of condemnation after Lauren's death and bring comfort to others. In the same manner, the Holy Spirit wants to use you to comfort those who are hurting. Healing has its perfect way when we give of ourselves.

As I surrender to the Lord, the things of this world that I am missing with my daughter hold no comparison with my accomplishments that have eternal rewards. Truly I made the choice to serve God, regardless of the hardships, before the tree limb fell.

Now is the time for you to make your choice. If you choose to surrender to God completely, you'll find these last days before Christ's return to be the most fulfilling. On the other hand, if you choose to dwell on your past hurts, then you will spend your remaining days lacking joy and peace, waiting for Jesus to rescue you from this world.

10

Spiritual Warfare for Those Left Behind

From this moment on, you must purpose in your heart to walk in victory. You must desire to see God bring good from your situation. The choice is yours and no one can choose for you. Your pastor, spouse, counselor, or this author, cannot make the decision for you. I can promise you that Jesus is able to bring "beauty for ashes" (Isaiah 61:3). It is a covenant promise that He suffered for, thereby insuring your deliverance. You have a part in receiving the victory. First, you must live according to God's Word. Secondly, the Holy Spirit is the One who must lead you into all truth. Finally, you must believe the Word and not your feelings or other people's experiences.

If you are ready to be free from sorrow and grief, then read on. You must purpose in your heart to be delivered from sorrow and grief, then what I'm about to tell you will set you free.

When Jesus suffered all the torment of Calvary, He saw you. He knew that Satan would one day try to destroy you with grief and sorrow. Therefore, He paid the price in full so that the spirits of sorrow and grief would have no power in your life:

> He (Jesus) is despised and rejected by men, A Man of sorrows and acquainted with grief. And we hid, as it were, our faces from Him; He was despised, and we did not esteem Him.
>
> Surely, He has borne our griefs and carried our sorrows; . . .
>
> Isaiah 53:3-4

Write this Scripture down, post it on your mirror, place it on the refrigerator, believe this Word is for you. Jesus carried your sorrow. Therefore, you don't have to have it. After my daughter died, well-meaning Christian friends and pastors waited and watched for sorrow and grief to overtake me. Many orally acknowledged that grief was inevitable. Some went as far as to tell me that I was in denial.

However, I have learned to search the Scriptures for the answers. When everyone told me that my sister's baby would die, I discovered that the Word declared that by the stripes of Jesus (Isaiah 53:5) baby Andrew would be healed.

This was no different. The Lord knows that I was willing to wear black and cry with the best of them, if that would have brought glory to His name. I knew that Jesus wanted me to be whole and full of His joy. Did He really pay a price high enough to eliminate the suffering that others knew I had to endure?

As I cried out to the Lord for truth, He led me to that beautiful Scripture in Isaiah and asked me if I wanted this sorrow and grief. When I said no, He assured me that He had borne it so that I did not have to. I thanked Him and will continue to thank Him. My well-meaning friends were wrong, because we don't have to suffer with grief.

I asked the Lord why I had only suffered from grief and sorrow those first few hours after the people had left our home. The intense pain I experienced was indescribable. He reminded me that when I had awakened that first night, I began to thank and praise Him that Lauren was in heaven. Seeing God's perspective on a saint's homecoming helped me to be able to praise the Lord.

The Lord instructed me to turn to Isaiah 35:10. It states: "They shall obtain joy and gladness, And sorrow and sighing shall flee away." The Lord then lead me to Isaiah 51:11 and again I read: "They shall obtain joy and gladness; Sorrow and sighing shall flee away."

The Lord went on to explain that I should not be concerned just because I had received His joy the first night and did not sorrow for a long time. His joy was so powerful that sorrow and grief had to flee.

If you are ready to see grief and sorrow destroyed in your situation, then submit to God. Begin to praise Him for destroying the works of the devil (1 John 3:8). Submission to God means aligning your thoughts with His Word. He said that His Son carried this pain for you—thank Him and praise Him for such a great truth. Now that you realize that you do not have to feel so horrible, I pray that a holy anger against the enemy will stir you. Then you will be a vessel used mightily by God. Satan has no authority to steal from you, therefore, determine that it will not happen again. Ask God to forgive you for allowing erroneous doctrine to hinder your victory. Start walking in the victory that Christ won for you.

I would be lying if I let you believe that Satan will not attack you again. That's the time to put all your warfare knowledge to use to win the battles that come against you. The battles will take place in your mind. The devil will bring terrible thoughts to you concerning the death of your loved one, and even speak to you through the mouths of others—some of them Christians. When that happens, remember:

> For though we walk in the flesh, we do not war according to the flesh.
>
> For the weapons of our warfare are not carnal but mighty in God for pulling down strongholds,
>
> casting down arguments and every high thing that exalts itself against the knowledge of God, bringing every thought into captivity to the obedience of Christ,
>
> and being ready to punish all disobedience when your obedience is fulfilled.
>
> 2 Corinthians 10:3-6

The Word of God must be more real to you than your circumstance. I remember shopping for Christmas presents six months after Lauren's death; as I entered the toy store, beautiful dolls seemed to taunt me. Satan whispered in my ear that I could no longer buy dolls for my little girl. I cast that thought down and spoke quietly to myself: "The dolls on this shelf cannot compare with the treasures of heaven. Lauren will celebrate Christmas with Jesus. How wonderful for her to celebrate His birthday in His presence." Just to kick the devil in the teeth, I bought a doll for myself. Not only that, I can buy as many dolls as I like and share them with little girls who might not know the love of Jesus.

You must learn to take every thought captive and speak the truth from God's perspective. We must be willing to have our minds renewed in the Word. Our only hope for wholeness lies in being transformed into the image of Christ. As Christians many of us say the right things, but now we must begin to live the crucified life. The illusions of this world quickly shatter when tragedy occurs. However, the crucified life is where true love, joy, and peace are found. As you emerge victorious from this journey, you shall fall so completely in love with Jesus that, like Paul, you will count the trials and tribulations as rubbish (Philippians 3:8). Nothing will compare to the glory that Christ desires to reveal in you.

I encourage you to find some good books on spiritual warfare. Read books by teachers who know the power of the Cross. Let the Holy Spirit lead you into deeper understanding. The

Joy Comes in the Morning

Scriptures in this book are meant to help you get started on your road to victory; however, nothing is more exciting than when the Holy Spirit gives you fresh manna from heaven. Ask Him today to give you new revelation as you read the Bible.

11

What Now?

If you have suffered the loss of a loved one and you want victory over the sorrow and grief, please use these biblical truths to win your battle:

1. This is the most difficult truth to receive because of our human pride: If you consider the tragedy to be God's will, you then need to repent of that. Once we humble ourselves, God will pour out His grace. As long as we continue to believe that the Lord purposed for our tragedy to happen, then we are hindering our ability to receive the grace needed for healing. God is not the author of evil. James declares that, "Every good gift and every perfect gift is from above, and comes down from the Father of lights, with whom there is no variation or shadow of turning" (James 1:17).

2. Seek God for comfort. We mustn't blame Him for our tragedy. Instead, allow Him to reveal the reasons behind your situation. Never let the enemy bring condemnation into your heart for the tragedy that occurred: "There is therefore now no condemnation to those who are in Christ Jesus, who do not walk according to the flesh, but according

to the Spirit" (Romans 8:1). *As God reveals the truth about your situation,* your healing will begin: "And you shall know the truth, and the truth shall make you free" (John 8:32).

3. Talk about the death of your loved one with someone possessing like faith. You may not be able to think of anything else for quite a while. Do not think that others don't want to hear how you feel. It may help to talk about the circumstances with others. As time passes, the need to talk about the person and the tragedy will decrease, though it may never completely cease. Do not suppress the need to deal with the pain.

4. Do not become angry with God. Satan loves for us to be angry with our only true source of comfort. Anger hinders our ability to receive grace. Be angry at Satan; he is the one trying to destroy you: "The thief does not come except to steal, and to kill, and to destroy" (John 10:10).

5. Read the Bible.

6. Play praise tapes.

7. I found it helpful to read books about heaven. When you realize that heaven is much like the earth, minus all the destruction, then you will understand that a glorious reunion awaits you. Some of the books I recommend are:

I Saw Heaven by Roberts Liardon

Paradise the Holy City and the Glory of the Throne by Rev. Elwood Scott

Within Heaven's Gate by Rebecca Springer

Didn't You Read My Book? by Dr. Richard Eby

Catching a Glimpse of Heaven by E. M. Bounds

Little Ones To Him Belong by Gwen Shaw (highly recommended for children)

8. Do not hold onto material items in such a way as to make a shrine for the loved one. God is your only source of comfort and healing. Anything else would be a counterfeit and could become an idol. I am not suggesting that all the deceased person's items be given away; however, be careful not to acquire a dependency on these things.

I treated my daughter's clothes in the same manner I would have if she had outgrown them. The ones that were usable by her siblings, I kept. The remainder of her clothes went to relatives and friends. Because the Lord has healed my broken heart, I enjoy watching my niece wear Lauren's clothes. In the same manner, the toys that the boys could still play with, we let them have. We use a few of Lauren's favorite dolls for decorations.

I would like to warn you of a counterfeit experience that Satan tries to bring to many during their most vulnerable time. He makes you think that you can hear or see that loved one again while on this earth. Now I will not deny the possibility of the Lord giving you a spiritual blessing such as the vision I had of my daughter. I did not, however, ask for a vision nor did I seek a supernatural experience. Everything that occurred lined up with the Word. Furthermore, the Holy Spirit has used that vision to comfort many.

I want you to know that our citizenship is in the same kingdom as our departed, saved, loved one:

"Now, therefore, you are no longer strangers and foreigners, but fellow citizens with the saints and members of the household of God" (Ephesians 2:19); however, the voice of the Holy Spirit is our only connection with heaven: "For through Him we both have access by one Spirit to the Father" (Ephesians 2:18). A demonic spirit may imitate your loved one: "And no wonder! For Satan himself transforms himself into an angel of light" (2 Corinthians 11:14). Its mission is to deceive you into believing that God will bless you with visits from your loved one. These visits may seem comforting at first, but the end result will be confusion and pain. Please seek godly counsel if you feel that your loved one is readily accessible to you.

9. As soon as possible we watched videos of Lauren and looked through the photo albums. If Satan tries to make you feel as if it would be too painful to look at photos or videos, then pray the Scripture: "I can do all things through Christ who strengthens me" (Philippians 4:13). Do not allow fear to rule in your life. Stand firm with the Word of God and face your fears so that they don't rule you and destroy your joy.

10. Speak often of your loved one. They are still a part of your life, though unreachable until the soon return of Christ. My boys ask the Lord to give Lauren a kiss for them each night as they say their prayers. Some may wonder if this is scriptural, but God's Word says: "And whatever you ask in My name, that I will do, that the Father may be glorified in the Son. If you ask anything in My name, I will do it" (John 14:13-14).

11. Because it is so easy to remember the virtues of the deceased loved one, you must be careful not to exalt them in such a way as to cause confusion for the ones left behind. Some of the surviving siblings have told me how impossible it was to live up to the image of their brother or sister. Deep wounds result when parents do not allow the Holy Spirit to direct them. Remember, no one is perfect or Christ would not have died for us all.

12

How to Minister to Someone Who is Suffering From Sorrow

1. The anointing of the Holy Spirit must empower you, if you are to minister successfully. Your standard for Godly counsel must be the Word of God. Sharing personal experiences, which reinforce what the Bible teaches, is acceptable.

2. As a friend or relative of the person in need of comforting, it is important that you understand that the deceased person is constantly on the mind of your friend. It helps if you let them talk about that person and the circumstances surrounding their loved one's death. The deceased person may be the main topic of conversation for months to come—be patient and understanding.

3. As time goes on, it is important to remember the deceased person in your conversations with your friend. I tell people to think of it as you would if the person had gone to another country—after all, our citizenship is in heaven. Therefore, you still mention them at the appropriate times. Heaven is another place and it is just as real as where you are living. It is

difficult if time goes on and no one seems to remember the loved one; therefore, I strongly urge you to bring up the person's name to your friend. It helps to know that others remember your loved one.

4. Greatly appreciated are the cards and letters you send during the days immediately following a death. John and I read every card. The personal messages brought much needed support.

5. The many people who came to the viewing and funeral were a great source of support. We didn't get to greet all those who attended; nevertheless, seeing a large number of caring people encouraged our hearts. Later, while looking over the guest books, we were encouraged by the names written there.

6. Bring food, and help with daily chores as needed; it is very difficult to deal with daily duties for a few weeks.

7. Immediately following the death, it is best to keep your doctrine to yourself. Let the Holy Spirit direct your conversation—He will always minister in love. Spiritual pride or fear should not be a motivational factor in your conversation. Please allow the Holy Spirit time to reveal His truth to those who are hurting.

8. We appreciated the books and tapes on heaven that people shared with us. (See the previous chapter for titles of helpful books.)

9. To know that the Lord was bringing souls into the kingdom through Lauren's death was the greatest encouragement. Therefore, we rejoiced that $1,400 was raised for missionaries in memory of our daughter.

10. Flowers placed on the loved one's grave, months after the funeral, bring joy to the hearts of the

immediate family. It is encouraging knowing that others still remember our daughter.

11. Let the Holy Spirit lead you as you continually keep your friend in prayer. Holidays and birthdays are especially difficult for the ones left behind—pray during these times.

13

For With God Nothing Will be Impossible

If you are facing a tragic situation and you feel that it is impossible to glorify God, then I pray that the following list of good things that He brought forth from my daughter's death will encourage you. With each new day the list grows; therefore, I have included just a small sample.

My brother, Lewis Pearce Jr., gave his life to the Lord. His wife, Wanda, rededicated her life to Jesus. Also, other relatives and friends have given their lives to the Lord. We anticipate that many others who attended the funeral will eventually be saved.

One of our neighbors confided in me that her stepson had died a few years earlier. When she saw my faith in Christ, she then believed for the healing of her own pain.

One month after the accident, John and I gave our testimony at the Poquoson Assembly of God church. It was a miracle that my husband and I were ministering together. After the loss of a child, the percentage of marriages that end in divorce is extremely high (I have heard estimations as high as 75%). Instead, God was taking us into a deeper sphere of commitment both to Him and to one another.

A few months had passed since the accident and I was delivering coupon books to one of my fund raising clients. She had heard about my situation. As I entered her home, she voiced her deep sympathy over my loss. She explained that, five years ago, her son was hit by a tree branch and sustained massive head injuries. Although he is a grown man, she has to care for him as if he were an infant. She is responsible for his every need. I commented on how difficult it must be caring for him, and that I felt that in many ways she needed more grace from God for her situation than I did for mine. Suddenly, she became very bitter and declared that she no longer believed all this "God stuff." She could not understand why her son was injured, but she had thanked the Lord that his life was spared. Then, two years later, she learned that her older son had perished in a fire.

When her pastor did not have the answers to help her, she felt that God was punishing her. Therefore, she completely walked away from the Lord.

The Holy Spirit gently prompted me to share the vision I had of Lauren in heaven. I explained that the Lord did not try to destroy her family. According to John 10:10, Satan is the one responsible for attacking her sons. I told her to read the Gospels and discover what a loving Jesus we serve. Peace flooded her spirit; hope filled her heart. While hugging me, she thanked me for telling her the truth. Tears were streaming down my face as I returned to my van. The Holy Spirit was using me to bring His lost and hurting sheep back into the fold.

The Lord instructed me to send a letter to a woman who had lost her young daughter when a drunk driver hit their car. Since the accident, six years prior to that time, sorrow and grief had made enjoying life impossible. Her strong belief in God was not enough to restore her joy. Only the truth from God's Word could heal this woman's broken heart. After receiving the letter concerning the truths God had taught me about Lauren's death, she began living again. The power of God has transformed her life.

Shortly after the Lord healed this woman, she was a tower of strength for her family during a crisis. The doctors held no hope for her mother's recovery from a stroke and other serious complications. However, because of this woman's faith and the faith of other family members, God miraculously healed her mother.

Ben Buchanan sought my help after the death of his son. He and his new bride, Jeanie, have become two of our dearest friends. The following is his testimony, written in his own words:

It was two in the morning, on a Saturday in late August of 1993, when I was awakened by several knocks on my door. A police officer gave me the message to call an Amtrak investigator in Maryland. Instantly, my body felt weak. I asked the officer if there had been an accident. She would not tell me.

Desperately, I tried repeatedly to contact the investigator but could not make the telephone connection. Next, I called the home of the friend my son, who was blind, was supposed to be visiting. I asked if I could speak to my son. The reply from the other end of the phone startled me. "Oh my God, you haven't heard that Chris has been killed in a terrible accident." He went on to tell me how my son became disoriented as he disembarked from the train. He accidentally stepped into the path of a moving train.

Day after day I continued to question God: Why did He allow my son to die? Why would He leave me all alone? How could a loving God remove His hand of protection from a twenty-six-year-old blind man? At the time, God seemed so distant that I questioned His existence.

Not knowing how to cope with the sorrow and grief, as well as the guilt, I began taking antidepressants. After a few days into the world of antidepressants my nervous system went out of control. I felt that death was the only way to ease the pain. The only thing I could think of was dying and going to heaven to be with Chris. Finally, the Holy Spirit broke through my pain and revealed that Satan had killed my son. Now Satan was trying to destroy me. Desperately, I called on God.

God led me to Cyndi Foster, who had lost her daughter in a freak accident just one year earlier. She described, in detail, the way that Satan had killed her daughter. I was amazed at how joyful and at peace she seemed as she talked of the tragedy. I saw the love of Jesus in her face. Likewise, her voice was full of compassion as she spoke of the greatness of God. At this point, I wanted what Cyndi had.

Though I left the Foster's home still grieving over my son's death, I was able to begin witnessing. A heart full of thanks replaced the bitterness that had tried to destroy me. By getting into God's will, my healing was underway.

(Ben was healed by the grace of God. He serves God as a missionary both abroad and at home. You'll find him and his new bride witnessing wherever they go. The joy has returned to his life!)

A friend of mine connected me with her childhood friend who had lost her husband and daughter in an automobile collision with

a drunk driver. She alone walked away from the vehicle. Just weeks before the fatal accident her husband and daughter had given their lives to the Lord. It was wonderful to be a vessel used by God to encourage this young woman with the assurance that she would see her husband and daughter again in heaven.

The most unusual way God has used my testimony happened while I was grocery shopping. As I pushed my cart to my van, a man in his early thirties approached me. He obviously hadn't taken a bath for a few days. His unkempt appearance was an indicator that I should continue with caution. He asked if he could help me unload my groceries. I told him not to bother because I could handle it myself. He then taunted me for being frightened by him. At this point, the anointing of God fell upon me. Looking him directly in the eye, I informed him that he did not intimidate me.

Astonished by my boldness, he asked me what I was "packing." He went further to mention the brands of some handguns. I told him that what I carried with me was much more powerful than a gun. Now I really had his attention.

"Lady, what have you got?" he earnestly wanted to know.

"I've got Jesus," I said.

He began to laugh and holy anger came over me. I looked him squarely in the face and demanded that he not laugh at my Jesus. I told him of my daughter's death and of the Lord's faithfulness to me. Suddenly, tears welled up in his eyes. He told me that at one time he did know the Lord, however, his cocaine addiction had destroyed his walk with the Lord. He asked me to pray for him. Right there, in the parking lot, I grabbed his hands and he repeated a prayer to the Lord after me. As I rebuked the spirit of cocaine, his countenance changed and his glassy eyes filled with tears of joy.

His dealer was waiting at his apartment to kill him if he returned without my money. He begged me to pray for his protection.

Just as quickly as this man appeared, he left. Two large men jumped in the car with him and off they sped. For fifteen minutes I interceded in the Holy Spirit. I know that God protected him.

I could list other testimonies of God bringing forth fruit from the seed (my daughter's life) laid down. Because the need is great, God called me to start Beauty For Ashes, Inc., "An Isaiah 61:1-3 Ministry."

Section Three

Defeated Foe

14

Call 911

Unrealistically, I felt that having survived a major tragedy would exclude me from walking through any future trials. However, the enemy does not follow our self-made rules. Only nine short months had passed since my daughter's accident and now our family was facing another major crisis.

Mitchell's teacher called to inform us that the chickenpox virus was running rampant through the school. Though I knew all the principles of spiritual warfare, I never seriously rebuked the illness as our six-year-old son began to break out with spots. When he did, I remembered what the Holy Spirit had said to me a year before as I watched little Nicolas die in my arms: "Do not allow the enemy to have a foothold in Mitchell's life—if given an inch he'll take a mile." That mile had begun.

Almost immediately, Mitchell was feverish and lethargic. Within twenty-four hours, his speech was incoherent. I was up all Saturday night watching and contemplated taking him to the hospital. Finally he went to sleep. John awoke and went to church. When he came home, I told him how concerned I was about Mitchell. He went in to take a look. At the very moment that John looked in on his son, Mitchell went into a convulsion. His eyes rolled back into his head and his arms flung about uncontrollably.

"Cyndi, dial 911 and pray!" yelled John.

I dialed the number and then handed the telephone to John and began to intercede in the Spirit. He informed the dispatcher of Mitchell's condition. The ambulance was on the way. Meanwhile, Mitchell had stopped convulsing and his speech returned to normal. Nevertheless, once the rescue workers arrived and checked my son's vital signs, their concern was obvious. They bundled Mitchell into blankets and carried him to the ambulance.

My husband grabbed his jacket and rushed out the door. He didn't want our son to arrive at the hospital without one of us being there. Michael, who had just turned three, was crying in my arms. He didn't want those people to take his brother away in that ambulance. The image of the ambulance coming to our house for his sister was still fresh in his mind. I reassured him that this was different; Mitchell would be coming back home. While standing in my hallway holding Mitchell's frightened little brother, I heard the Holy Spirit speaking to my heart. I *knew* that Mitchell would be healed. There was no waiting on the Lord this time and no need to hide in my prayer closet. I knew that the Holy Spirit was promising me that my son would not die.

I waited patiently for John to return with our son. I thought that the convulsions were symptoms of a high fever. How could a simple childhood illness such as chickenpox cause anyone to need hospitalization? I jumped as the telephone interrupted my thoughts—John was calling to inform me of the severity of our son's condition. With despair in his voice, he went on to tell me that the physicians believed that Mitchell was suffering from Reye's Syndrome. Reye's Syndrome occurs mainly in children and usually follows a viral infection such as chickenpox or influenza. The origin of Reye's Syndrome is unknown, but in rare instances it occurs when aspirin is administered to children with viral infections. I assured John that I had never given our children aspirin. The diagnosis was not definite and additional tests had to be given to our son. John told me that Mitchell wanted me to come and hold his hand.

As I was hanging up the phone, the doorbell rang. My neighbor and good friend, Marti Lucento, and her daughter, Amber, wanted to know what was wrong. Amber had seen the ambulance carrying Mitchell away. They both had tears in their eyes. Because we're both good friends and neighbors, our children are constantly together. When Lauren died they also felt a great loss. Now the thought of possibly losing Mitchell tore at their hearts.

After explaining all that had transpired, I asked them to look after Michael so that I could go to the hospital. They took my distraught little boy home with them. I was in no condition to drive to the hospital, so I called my brother-in-law, Doug Livermon, and he agreed to take me. As I waited for Doug to reach my house, I prayed and asked the Lord to give me direction. The Holy Spirit very clearly told me that this affliction was not going to end in death. I remember telling the Lord that I hadn't thought this was going to end with any hospitalization—after all, this was childhood chickenpox. Every child handles this virus by staying home for ten days and driving their mothers crazy! Mitchell should not have been in the hospital.

The drive to the hospital was very quiet—I was seeking guidance from the Holy Spirit. The Lord would only impress one thought on my heart: *Submit to John, and I will instruct him.*

As I entered the emergency room, I observed that Mitchell was surrounded by medical personnel who seemed greatly concerned over his condition. Apprehension was seeping into my spirit. I needed to hear from the Lord from His Word. I opened my Bible. My eyes looked at the verse that lay before me:

> See that you are not troubled; for all things must come to pass, but the end is not yet.
>
> Matthew 24:6

I knew that this verse deals with end time events, however, the Holy Spirit was giving me this promise for my particular situation. Just as the Lord had spoken to my heart before I left my home, now He was confirming that our family would walk through another trial. The result of this trial would be life, not death.

They had put an IV in my frightened little boy's arm and were preparing him to undergo a brain scan. Clinging to me, he begged me to take him home. He tried to get up off the bed and leave. I promised him a pool table (I meant the children's version, though his dad bought a real pool table!) if he would cooperate with the doctors. I whispered to him that Jesus would heal him. While waiting for the tests to come back, I sang Bible promises to Mitchell.

The staff neurologist explained that the medical tests had revealed that a virus was attacking Mitchell's brain, causing it to swell. At this point, they believed that Reye's Syndrome was the culprit. The technical name for this condition is encephalitis, which is untreatable except for the herpes simplex virus type one. The virus attacking Mitchell was not that type, so the doctor could only wait to see how far this deadly strain would go. Mitchell's chances for survival did not look good.

We needed to choose between allowing this small local hospital to treat our son or transferring him to a hospital with a Pediatric Intensive Care Unit (PICU). Though we felt confident with the hospital's neurologist, we prayed that the Lord would open the right doors for Mitchell's care. The local hospital informed us that they would transfer our son to a larger hospital because they had no beds in their intensive care unit. We felt that transferring Mitchell was the logical course of action. At this point, however, the doctor told us that a bed had suddenly become available and so the transfer wasn't necessary. We weren't sure if leaving our son in this facility was the best thing to do. John whispered to me that maybe we should move Mitchell to a larger hospital anyway.

As we prayed for direction, a nurse strongly recommended we transfer Mitchell to a hospital equipped to handle the severity of his condition. John knew that God was directing our steps. He asked that they transfer Mitchell to a hospital with a PICU. We still didn't know which of the two nationally known hospitals in our area would have an available bed. Instead of transferring Mitchell to one of the hospitals that specialize in pediatric care, they transferred Mitchell to a medium size facility on the outskirts of Richmond, Virginia.

A pediatric neurologist that we contacted agreed to take our case—his son-in-law was the neurologist who administered the tests on our son when we were in Williamsburg. Again we knew that God was in charge of all these details.

We signed the release forms as the transport unit from Richmond arrived. The staff gave us directions to the hospital. We were only minutes behind the transport unit. John and I were silent, lost in our own thoughts. After having buried one of our children just nine months earlier, it was inconceivable that our faith was being tested again. Every thought screamed of death for our son. The enemy wanted to cause me to doubt the promises of my God. It took every weapon of warfare that I had studied and taught to control my thoughts. I would not let fear fill my mind.

Instead, I concentrated on the goodness of God, the mercy of my Lord, the truth in His Word!

As I glanced up, I noticed that I had been on this exact stretch of highway before. The billboards were very familiar. Suddenly, I knew that we were headed for the very hospital where my friend's son had died just one year ago. *Lord, I see your hand in this, please don't make me believe for a miracle as great as what I wanted for Nicolas,* I thought. It was ironic that I had just finished writing the section of this book concerning Nicolas's death. I remembered just days before asking the Lord how people would see victory in my testimony? How could anyone be inspired to seek Him after reading my story? I felt as if the Lord was about to give me the ending for the book.

My thoughts raced back to a few nights earlier— to the church we attended on Wednesdays. As I rushed into the sanctuary, scanning the pews for my husband who had gone in ahead of me, I spotted Donna Fox. Five years ago, our families attended the same Bible study. John was sitting directly in front of her. I slipped into the pew next to him. Quietly, I turned and greeted Donna, then turned my attention to the praise and worship. John whispered that Donna had been diagnosed with an incurable cancer. Donna was thirty-three and had three small children. I was eager to minister to her, yet leery of becoming involved. I recalled the hurt and disappointment of holding little Nicolas as he died.

Just days after praying about ministering to Donna Fox,[1] I was driving to the same hospital where cancer had defeated me. God was about to show me His great healing power. It was as if the Spirit was telling me to get back up on the horse and ride. My flesh cringed at what lay ahead, however, my spirit knew that God was doing an awesome work.

Once we drove into the parking lot, all doubt vanished—this was the exact hospital where Nicolas had died. As we went down the corridor and entered the PICU, I saw the same people who had mocked my belief in a healing God almost exactly one year prior. I saw the bed where I had held Nicolas as his body ceased functioning.

We found Mitchell just three beds over in the isolation room of the same unit. After Mitchell was hooked up to the machines that monitored his illness and fed him intravenously, I told John that I would spend the night at the hospital. He went home to get some sleep. I then called Carla, Nicolas's mother, to let her know I was in town.

[1]Donna Fox has had no indications of cancer since being prayed for by Pastor Benny Hinn (as well as being completely obedient to the leading of the Holy Spirit).

15

Obedience to the Holy Spirit

Sam and Carla Arnold insisted that I spend the night with them since they lived only a few blocks from the hospital. Sam came to the hospital and drove me to their house. I was delighted to find that Carla had found a peace about Nicolas's death and was allowing the Holy Spirit to administer healing.

Carla and Sam had just learned that she was pregnant with their fourth child. She felt it was God's way of letting her get on with her life. We talked. The memory of Nicolas's death hung in the air. I felt that Sam was doubtful that I was delivered from sorrow and grief so quickly. He had visited us only once since the accident and didn't know of the daily victories in our lives. He questioned my ability to remain calm while my son was critically ill. However, I couldn't pretend that I was worried, for the Lord had reassured me with His Word. I knew that Mitchell would be healed.

Around midnight I went to bed. Their guest bed looked inviting because I hadn't slept for two nights. I was about to fall asleep but the Holy Spirit very gently told me to go back to the hospital. At first I thought this must be my own thought; after all, why would God not allow me to have this wonderful, much needed rest? I knew that my flesh wouldn't choose to go outside in the freezing weather, so I was certain the voice telling me to return to the hospital was the voice of the Holy Spirit. As I was dressing to return to the hospital, I prayed that the Lord would awaken Sam. I did not have the heart to wake him at this late hour. As I walked down the stairs, I saw him sitting on the couch still wide awake.

"Sam, I hate to ask you to take me back to the hospital, but I really need to be there," I said.

"Carla and I are really worried about you," Sam said. "No matter how much you trust the Lord, you're still human. You must be worried. Please stay and get some rest."

He encouraged me to call first and see how Mitchell was doing, but the condition of my son was irrelevant. I had to obey the Holy Spirit, and that meant returning to the hospital. Sam agreed to drive me. Silently, we headed toward our destination.

When we got there, Sam asked if he could go with me to the intensive care unit. Since Nicolas's death, neither he nor Carla had returned to the unit. Because of his concern for me, he was willing to go to a place that still held strong and painful memories.

Upon entering an intensive care unit, it is natural to dread seeing the entire medical staff hovering over your loved one. As we entered the unit, we noticed that all the medical personnel were surrounding Mitchell. They looked very concerned as they explained that my son had just had a serious convulsion. Sam had a sad look on his face. The convulsion didn't worry me, though. (Circumstances play no part in determining the reactions of those who walk by faith.) As Sam stood beside me, I opened my Bible. The Holy Spirit directed me to read the Scripture aloud:

> And as he was still coming, the demon threw him down and convulsed him. Then Jesus rebuked the unclean spirit, healed the child, and gave him back to his father.
>
> Luke 9:42

With renewed confidence, I read the Scripture to Sam again. God knew about the convulsion and declared through that passage that Mitchell would be healed and returned to my husband. My instructions from the Holy Spirit remained unchanged: I was to submit to John while holding fast to my promise for Mitchell's healing.

I spent the next few hours trying to sleep on a small cot in the waiting room. Sleep eluded me, however, so I prayed. (My time with the Lord strengthens me in ways sleep never could.) At six-thirty in the morning, I went into Mitchell's room and spent most of the day watching him. He was so sick and frightened. Hundreds of chickenpox blisters covered his frail body. The dried pus from the blisters practically glued his eyes shut. Drinking was impossible because of the swelling of his tongue. He was miserable.

After all the test results were back from the lab, the specialist assigned to my son, concluded that Mitchell's illness was not a result of Reye's Syndrome. The doctors deduced that Mitchell's immune system had completely shut down. This allowed the varicella-zoster virus, which belongs to the herpes virus family and is the cause of chickenpox, to enter my son's major organs. What had happened in Mitchell's body was virtually unheard of in a healthy child. Though none of the doctors involved had ever treated a case like Mitchell's, they had heard of children on chemotherapy having such an attack because their immune systems were vulnerable. The occurrence of the virus attacking the major organs is extremely rare.

The next twenty-four hours were critical. If the virus continued in its attack against Mitchell's major organs, his chance for survival would be slim. Already the tests revealed that major brain damage had occurred—if Mitchell lived through this brutal attack, he would require extensive therapy to function again. At this point, one nurse advised me to consider renting an apartment in Richmond. She wanted to make sure that I understood that the Mitchell Foster who was admitted to the hospital days before, would not be the same child that would leave the intensive care unit. My son would die at the hands of this virus or he would return to us mentally and physically impaired. I never let the report enter my spirit, nor did I tell anybody of the prognosis.

I spent the day just watching Mitchell. The Lord had told me to submit to John. The Lord did not want me to get all spiritual in the hospital room. I was instructed to trust the Lord and allow my husband to fight this battle. Oh, how important it is to hear the voice of the Lord. We are so very dependent on the Spirit for all the promises in the Word—and our submission to them. That's the sum of our responsibility concerning the promises of God. It's much easier to turn to formulas and to do the "spiritual things." Nevertheless, we are called to die to ourselves and submit to His will. This time, I was obeying the Spirit by just watching my son and believing that Jesus was going to heal him.

John arrived at the hospital around dinner time. He was planning to stay with Mitchell until eleven that night and then return before his son awoke in the morning. I decided not to mention what the doctor had told me about our son's condition. I just left, knowing that God would instruct John as to the next step.

Around ten that night, while on his evening rounds, Mitchell's doctor approached my husband. Since he had spoken with me that morning, additional tests had shown that extensive damage had taken place in Mitchell's body. John was told the terrible news. He called me from the hospital to inform me of the devastating report. He didn't go into detail, but he mentioned that Mitchell's liver was not functioning. We would have to make some major medical decisions soon.

How dare the defeated foe try to destroy my son! I had just finished listening to a teaching tape in which the speaker said that the head of the household must take authority over the enemy, which confirmed what the Holy Spirit told me that John was to do. Jesus gave us the authority to defeat the attacks of the enemy:

> Behold, I give you authority to trample on serpents and scorpions, and over all power of the enemy, and nothing shall by any means hurt you.
>
> Luke 10:19

I told John that if he commanded Satan to take his hands off our son, then Satan had to obey. John had heard teaching on the power of the blood of Jesus and the name of Jesus. My husband knew in his spirit that he was the one who had to take authority over the enemy attacking our son's body. After everyone left Mitchell's room, my husband asserted his blood-bought authority over the virus that was destroying our son's major organs. At that time there was no visible sign that the situation had changed. However, we must learn to walk by faith and not by sight (2 Corinthians 5:7).

John arrived home after midnight. Although exhausted from the long hours at the hospital, he felt inclined to share with me the terrible news concerning our son. Up to this point, he had not spoken the bad report to anyone. The Holy Spirit had informed me of the report and directed me not to speak it forth. Though my flesh wanted desperately to talk about the attack against Mitchell, I knew the spiritual danger of asking John to speak out the report to me. I told him to pray about telling me, since he hadn't told a soul— maybe it was better not to speak out what the enemy was trying to do. I was not going to receive a bad report anyway. John decided to wait until morning before telling me. He needed time to pray and get direction from the Lord.

16

The Prayer of Faith

After everyone was asleep, I went to my prayer closet. Sitting on the floor, feeling absolutely helpless, I cried out to God. He was going to heal my son. I never questioned the healing, though I didn't know the specifics. As I lifted my hands toward heaven, I told the Lord that I knew that I could not do a single thing for my own son. In me there was nothing to give—it was all the work of the Holy Spirit. In and of ourselves there is no power, but through Christ who dwells in us, there is resurrection power: "I can do all things through Christ who strengthens me" (Philippians 4:13).

As I cried out to the Lord, a very powerful presence of God filled the atmosphere. The Lord spoke so clearly to my heart that audible words would not have penetrated any stronger. He distinctly instructed me to ask anything believing, without doubting, and it would be done for me, exactly as I asked. He told me to be specific:

> For assuredly, I say to you, whoever
> says to this mountain, 'Be removed and
> be cast into the sea,' and does not doubt
> in his heart; but believes that those things
> he says will be done, he will have
> whatever he says.
>
> Therefore I say to you, whatever
> things you ask when you pray, believe
> that you receive them and you will have
> them.
>
> Mark 11:23-24

The impact of the Lord's command brought tears of joy to my eyes. Very cautiously, I made my request to the Lord: *Lord, I want my son healed completely. I want it to be an instantaneous healing with absolutely no long term treatment required. Lord, I do not want his brain to be damaged. I do not want him to have a liver transplant. Finally, Lord, I want him home within a few days.*

While speaking my request, I could feel the power of God upon me. Now I knew the specifics of God's healing for my son. There would be no need to rent an apartment in Richmond because God would reverse the brain damage. Moreover, my son would not need a liver transplant or any other corrective surgery. I knew that the same little boy I had held in my arms just last week would be the same child God would return to me. We were going to experience an undeniable miracle!

Before I could share with John the promise the Holy Spirit had given me, he was on his way to the hospital. Wanting to be with Mitchell when he awoke, my husband arose early; therefore, he did not have time to tell me the horrible news the doctor had given him just last night.

Mitchell's doctor called me at home just minutes after John left for the hospital. He told me that something astounding had taken place during the night. For some medically unexplainable reason, Mitchell's immune system had mysteriously fought off the virus. To the amazement of the medical staff, my son's permanently damaged brain had completely healed itself during the night. His lungs no longer showed any signs of ever being attacked by the deadly virus. Furthermore, his liver that had completely ceased to function, had begun to perform properly.

I told the doctor that we had been praying that God would give him wisdom to treat our son.

He replied that he didn't know if I understood the severity of our child's illness, that they did not have any treatment for the virus that was attacking his major organs and that they were helpless to do anything except keep him comfortable. Then he said, in effect, "Please don't give any credit to me or my staff. What happened with your son did not come from us."

"Are you telling me, as a medical doctor, that I got a miracle?" I asked overwhelmed by this man's honesty.

He laughed and said that he was just saying that our son was fine and they can't take the credit.

"When a medical doctor says you've gotten a miracle, then you've gotten a miracle," I said.

Before the call came, I had already expected God to heal Mitchell completely. However, I was delighted that this medical professional would give God all the glory. It takes a physician of strong integrity to humble himself and admit that a higher power is involved.

To celebrate my son's miracle, I called everyone with the good news. Our pastor, who had returned from his vacation, was thrilled. Everyone I spoke to was given the wonderful testimony that my son was healed by the power of the Most High God! I encouraged everyone to continue to pray and thank the Lord until Mitchell was home and completely healthy again.

As I waltzed into the hospital room, Mitchell's appearance shocked me. His swollen face made him unrecognizable. The damage to his liver had caused his skin to look yellowish.

"It's a good thing the doctor told us that he was in full recovery," I commented to John.

"What are you talking about?" he asked.

"Didn't the doctor and nurses tell you that Mitchell was miraculously healed last night?" I replied.

My husband had spent the entire day looking at Mitchell in this ghastly condition, never knowing that inside his body the healing had manifested itself. He didn't believe me at first. He thought that I had misunderstood the doctor. Maybe I was just speaking in faith.

Exhausted from the long day, John just could not wait any longer to speak to the doctor. As he walked out of the hospital room, he had a glimmer of hope in his heart. Maybe, just maybe, his wife had understood the doctor.

As I settled down to spend the night with my son, the nurses informed me that Mitchell had some visitors at the door. Because our son was in the intensive care unit, only the immediate family could come into his room. I had no idea who would make the hour drive to Richmond besides our immediate family. To my surprise, Mitchell's Royal Ranger leaders from church had felt compelled to come and pray for him. I warned them that Mitchell's face was swollen and discolored, however, I also assured them of the miracle that the Lord had performed in the early morning hours. This good report delighted them. Mitchell's healing was the result of many believers praying in faith for the enemy to be defeated. Churches throughout our community could share in the joy of knowing that their prayers were answered.

I spent the night on the little cot in the waiting room. Though the devil tried to convince me that I had misunderstood the doctor, I knew that Satan was just acting desperately in his attempt to destroy my joy.

Being with Mitchell Wednesday morning confirmed that prayers were answered. He was grumpy and upset by all the tubes attached to his body. This was a good sign for, up to this point, my little six-year old had not been responsive, even to painful stimuli. Now that he was healed, he was not pleased with the routine medical procedures.

Now that the internal healing had taken place, I began asking God for the smaller miracles. I asked God to heal the blisters on Mitchell's eyes so that he could see. Within hours the blisters disappeared from his eyes! Next, I asked the Lord to take the blisters out of my son's mouth so that he could eat and drink. Within hours those blisters disappeared.

John arrived around four in the afternoon. He had to admit that Mitchell looked much better than he had the day before. I told him that the doctor had not made his rounds yet. John was very eager to hear for himself the miraculous turn around. Though physically exhausted, I wanted to attend the Wednesday night service at church. Because John had not talked to the doctor, he wasn't 100% convinced that our son was in full recovery. Intellectually he couldn't comprehend that Mitchell was instantly healed. In his heart he longed for the doctor to confirm what his wife was saying. He knew that I wasn't the one who heard the doctor say that Mitchell had permanent brain damage and liver damage. After all, *he* was the one informed that the virus was attacking Mitchell's lungs. Maybe I just misunderstood what the doctor was telling me. Because of his uncertainty, John asked me not to mention Mitchell's healing to anyone until he had a chance to confirm it with the doctor.

17

The Lies

During the drive home, the enemy wasted no time in attacking my thoughts. He accused me of disobeying my husband. After all, I had told everyone about Mitchell's miracle before I had seen John. I knew that more than one church would be celebrating the healing with us that very night. Oppression hung over my spirit. Repeatedly the enemy whispered that I had disobeyed God by disobeying my husband. He reminded me of God's warning that I must submit to John. The Lord had warned me, from the very onset of this trial, that my place was to submit and allow God to work through my husband. By the time I arrived home, my joy had dissipated. Confusion and doubt, caused by the lies of the enemy, were defeating my strong faith.

In my heart I knew that I had to get to church. I called a dear friend, Dottie Hines, and asked her to drive me. Though she attended a different church, she said she would gladly take me anywhere I wanted to go. As I entered the sanctuary, the Holy Spirit began to minister to my heart. The pastor called out my name from the pulpit and asked about Mitchell. I told the congregation about the telephone call from the doctor. Everyone rejoiced over the good news.

As soon as I was seated, the enemy began to taunt me again. He told me how I had blown it with that testimony. He made me feel as if John would be furious that I didn't obey him. I had only told these people exactly what the doctor had said. John hadn't heard the doctor—I had. Just as doubt was fighting to overtake my faith, the pastor began to teach on the power of glorifying God during a trial. He spoke of the importance of praising the Lord until you see the promises of God happen in your situation. His words penetrated my heart. Satan's trap was exposed. Now I could see that the Holy Spirit wanted me to glorify the Lord. Satan did not want that glory to go forth. Submission is an attitude of the heart. By questioning my own actions I demonstrated my desire to be submissive to John. Now I was free to rejoice in the great miracle the Lord had done for our family!

Thursday was an uneventful day for our family. Mitchell was feeling more like his old self. Because he found the intensive care unit boring, he complained to all the staff. The true Mitchell Foster had emerged. The chickenpox blisters had scabbed over remarkably quickly. His eyes and tongue were now clear. He could eat for the first time in a week. The pediatric doctor on call was now his primary doctor. She could not understand how Mitchell pulled through his ordeal untouched, so she continued his antibiotic as a precaution. They were thrilled that somehow he beat the odds.

The news of Lauren's death nine months earlier had circulated in the PICU. Now that Mitchell's crisis was over, I had more time to witness concerning the grace of the Lord about Lauren. Several of the nurses left Mitchell's room with tears of conviction and the wonder of God in their eyes.

In the very early morning hours of Friday, I awoke to a gentle voice that I thought belonged to the Holy Spirit. This voice tried to persuade me to allow Mitchell to relapse, thereby allowing more people to be saved. The voice promised to bring my loved ones into the kingdom of God through the continuation of Mitchell's illness. I began to cry out to God to find another way. I just couldn't stand to have my son suffer for one moment longer. Nevertheless, my desire was to do the will of God, no matter what the cost. Just as I was entertaining this suggestion, the telephone rang with a shrill noise that pierced through the stillness. Could this be the hospital calling to inform me that my little boy had relapsed?

"Mom, it's me, Mitchell," came his quiet little voice. "When are you going to take me home?"

"Soon, baby, soon," I answered.

The nurse picked up the receiver and apologized for allowing Mitchell to call so early in the morning. She explained that he refused to take no for an answer.

As I hung up the phone, I immediately went downstairs to pray. I told the Lord that He had to find another way—Mitchell had been through enough. The Lord was faithful by allowing my son to call me in the middle of the night. The Holy Spirit knew what I needed to hear to stop me from listening to the lies of the enemy. Then I recognized the true voice of the Lord as He spoke to my heart.

He explained that He was not the One who would bring sickness on a little boy to save others. He told me that He was a loving God who takes what Satan means for evil and turns it to good. God would move mountains to save my loved ones—He didn't need to torment my son to bring forth salvation. Jesus endured torment for all of us almost two thousand years ago on the Cross. Now people only need to listen to the convicting voice of the Holy Spirit and surrender to God.

18

Beauty for Ashes

There was only one portion of my prayer that seemed impossible for God to answer: Get Mitchell home quickly. The doctor informed me Friday morning that my son had to finish his ten days of intravenously fed antibiotic. They predicted his release would take place in eight to ten days. I prayed silently that the Lord would have them forgo this requirement and discharge Mitchell sooner.

Mitchell longed to be home. He dreaded the morning routine of having his veins checked in order to find an appropriate one in which to insert the IV needle for the antibiotic drip. His veins were small and the best veins had collapsed due to the treatment. It was painful, for both my son and me, as they repeatedly stuck him while trying to insert the needle. Finally, the doctor was called. She has the reputation of being able to always insert the needle the first time, however, even she was poking the needle into vein after vein with no success. I cringed. Mitchell cried.

Then the peace of the Lord fell upon me. I whispered to Mitchell that I thought God was doing something special, and I encouraged him to hang in there. I then asked the doctor why she was making my son suffer for a treatment that she knew did not affect his condition. She agreed that if she didn't insert the needle in the next attempt, she would discontinue the procedure. Though the needle was carefully inserted, to the doctor's dismay, it was not positioned correctly. True to her word, she canceled the antibiotic treatment. Mitchell was released from the intensive care unit and transferred to a regular hospital room.

Seven days from the time we took Mitchell to the hospital, we took him home. He was weak but happy. I couldn't keep back the tears—partly for joy and partly from sorrow. Only one year ago I had left through these doors with a heavy heart, doubting my ability for God to ever use me again. Now I was beginning to understand the awesome power of God to transform us into the likeness of Jesus Christ so that we can do the works He did and change the world with the Gospel.

Through Jesus Christ and by the power of the Holy Spirit, God truly gives us "beauty for ashes and the oil of joy for mourning," when we stand fast in faith and obedience.

> The Spirit of the Lord GOD is upon Me,
> Because the LORD has anointed Me
> To preach good tidings to the poor;
> He has sent Me to heal the broken-hearted,
> To proclaim liberty to the captives,
> And the opening of the prison to those who are bound;

To proclaim the acceptable year of the LORD,

And the day of vengeance of our God;

To comfort all who mourn,

To console those who mourn in Zion,

To give them beauty for ashes,

The oil of joy for mourning,

The garment of praise for the spirit of heaviness;

That they may be called trees of righteousness,

The planting of the LORD, that He may be glorified.

Isaiah 61:1-3

19

The Ministry Continues

At the time I'm writing this it's been four years since the angels placed Lauren in the arms of the Lord Jesus Christ and three years since Mitchell fought his battle with death.

Since then, intense communion with the Holy Spirit has brought me into a powerful relationship with the Lord. The anointing of God is heavy upon my life and ministry. I truly love the Lord today with all my heart, soul, mind, and strength.

At the time of Lauren's death, I was learning the importance of a totally submitted life. Now my all consuming passion is to *know* Jesus Christ. Intimacy with the One who delivered me from my sorrow is my only desire. I have found that it never ends—this deeper understanding of Jesus Christ, the Holy Spirit, and the Father. Moving into this greater relationship of love with God has been worth the price of the hardships that I have encountered. The apostle Paul sums up my thoughts:

> But what things were gain to me,
> these I have counted loss for Christ.
>
> Yet indeed I also count all things loss
> for the excellence of the knowledge of
> Christ Jesus my Lord, for whom I have
> suffered the loss of all things, and count
> them as rubbish, that I may gain Christ
>
> and be found in Him, not having my
> own righteousness, which is from the
> law, but that which is through faith in
> Christ, the righteousness which is from
> God by faith; . . .
>
> Philippians 3:7-9

In October of 1995 I went to Russia, which proved to be the most rewarding of my ministry experiences since Lauren's death. Lauren had a burden for Russia. She had even saved up her allowance to send Bibles to children in that country. Unlike Lauren, though, I had not felt a call to minister in that nation. Once the Lord directed me to go, I knew that Russia would change my life. The enemy, of course, had other plans. Satan was determined to stop the trip by preventing me from getting the money I needed.

Three weeks before the scheduled trip, I received a letter from the ministry that was sponsoring the event. They stated that they needed my two thousand dollars within three days. Suddenly, as I was reading this portion of the letter, *I went totally blind.* However, with the blindness came a peace that was overwhelming. I had no fear. I knew immediately that God was responsible for my lack of sight.

I also knew that my nonchalant attitude concerning the trip to Russia had grieved the Holy Spirit. The Holy Spirit revealed that Satan wanted to steal the faith I needed to obtain the money for the trip. Because I never really desired to go to Russia, I was sitting back and not activating the faith within me for the finances. I repented and the Lord began to unveil the plan He had for me in this far away country. The Holy Spirit wanted me to know that I was going to Russia no matter the circumstances. I needed to fight the good fight of faith to fulfill my destiny in Russia.

Rather than frightening me, the blindness caused faith to well up within my spirit. Now it was easy for me to believe for the money to materialize.

Before the Lord restored my sight, He asked me how I felt about the darkness. My response was one of sadness, because the darkness seemed so hopeless. Then as suddenly as my sight was taken, it was restored. "Go and bring the light into Russia," the Holy Spirit said to my heart.

The deadline for the money came and went. Then I received notice that the group that sponsored the trip was purchasing my ticket for me, even though I did not yet have the money, because they felt I was destined to go with them. I am thankful for a godly ministry that obeys the leading of the Holy Spirit, even when it doesn't make sense.

Every day, when the mail came, I would rush to the mailbox expecting a two thousand dollar check to be there. Day after day I was disappointed. I cried out to God to increase my faith, for I did not want to miss the will of God. He gave me an Old Testament

Scripture about fighting with a bow. The Holy Spirit revealed to me that I needed to get my bow. *Surely, God does not intend for me to buy a bow and arrow,* I thought. Because I needed further explanation of this revelation, I sought the Holy Spirit.

He explained that a bow is used to attack the enemy from a distance, whereas, the sword requires one to be upon his enemy. I knew that I had to get something that was *only* for the trip. I decided to purchase a gigantic piece of luggage on wheels.

Since we were only allowed one piece of luggage and I would have to maneuver it myself, I needed something large with sturdy wheels. As I entered the luggage shop with my birthday money in hand, I explained to the clerk that I was going to Russia. He was a backslidden Christian. My testimony and determination not to miss God's will convicted the clerk of his need to return to church. While talking with the clerk, a man came into the store to apply for a job. As he overheard our conversation, he too was convicted of his lack of zeal for the Lord. By actively attacking the enemy with my purchase of luggage, I knew that the money for the trip would come.

Three days before the plane departed for Russia, the money came through a totally unexpected source who insisted on never being identified.

As I waited at the airport for takeoff, I was amazed that I was going to Russia—a place where I had never wanted to go and now wanted to go more than anywhere else. We rushed through customs with medical supplies and Christian literature.

Once in Russia, the accommodations in the small villages we went to provided me with a real missionary experience. Being a picky eater made fasting during this trip a pleasure—I lost over ten pounds in my sixteen-day stay.

Three churches were started by our team. Over two thousand souls were saved and thousands of Bibles were distributed. In the personal ministry that I was able to do, the most rewarding experience I had was a visit to an orphanage. I was asked to share anything that God had placed on my heart. As I shared, in a way appropriate for the young children surrounding me, many of the adults on our ministry team were touched for I had not shared my testimony with them. After hearing of the love Lauren had for Jesus, forty children asked Jesus Christ into their hearts. It was wonderful to see God use me to reach children for His kingdom. Although she is in heaven, I feel Lauren was grinning from ear to ear as she cheered me on. I believe she is in that great cloud of witnesses (Hebrews 12:1) watching me glorify God through testifying of the grace of our Lord Jesus Christ.

During the drive back to our hotel, the evangelist who led our team, Dwight Jones, asked me to share my full testimony with them. I shared all that Jesus had done for my family and me. After sharing on the bus, other opportunities became available to teach the truths that I have shared in this book to others on the trip. Whether in the United States or halfway around the world, God's Word sets people free.

The greatest change that occurred in my life during the trip was the victory over the only fear that still held me after the loss of Lauren—the fear of not having material possessions. I found that my dependency on the Lord Jesus Christ is all I need. In Russia, we had no bathrooms or modern conveniences during the trips to the villages. I lived in the perfect will of God. The glory was awesome. I drew closer to the Lord than I had ever known was possible. I know now that whatever the world may go through before the return of Christ; His grace is sufficient. His glory will sustain us. He will meet our needs as we trust Him completely. My joy is dependent on only one thing— Jesus will never leave me nor forsake me.

The Beauty for Ashes, Inc., (BFA) ministry was founded in February 1995. God has ordained this ministry with both the anointing and an understanding of the deep truths of God. Revival takes place during our meetings. The Holy Spirit visits the people with great manifestations of power. Convictions and salvations take place in the presence of God. Lives have been changed. Many have repented and walked away from sinful habits. In the Book of Acts, signs and wonders followed the teaching of the Word—the same thing happens when the BFA ministry team is invited to minister in the full liberty of the Spirit of God.

Since last year, we have held women's conferences and marriage conferences. Women have been delivered from their past sins and hurts. Some of the healings occur in the areas of past abortions, affairs, sexual abuse, and other traumas that cause depression and suicide in women. The anointing given to the BFA ministry team accompanies the teaching of the Word. Together they bring total deliverance, restoration, or healing to many individuals. We have testimonies of suicides being prevented and fears and phobias eliminated. God has a message of victory for the last day saints. Our ministry is about finding victory.

Conferences, church meetings, revivals, and women's retreats are only some of the doors that the Holy Spirit is opening for our ministry.

If you feel that the Lord would have us share with your group or congregation, please contact us at 1-757-253-0390 or by writing to:

> Beauty for Ashes, Inc.
> P.O. Box 1209
> Williamsburg, VA 23187
> (757) 253-0390
> e-mail: btyfrashes@aol.com
> website: www.beautyforashes.org

Impac Chris ian Books

332 Leffingwell Ave., Suite 101
Kirkwood, MO 63122

AVAILABLE AT YOUR LOCAL BOOKSTORE, OR YOU MAY
ORDER DIRECTLY. Toll-Free, order-line only M/C, DISC,
or VISA 1-800-451-2708.

Visit our Website at *www. impactchristianbooks.com*

Write for *FREE* Catalog.